# DOCKER'S DAIMLERS

## DAIMLER AND LANCHESTER CARS
## 1945 TO 1960

# RICHARD TOWNSEND

AMBERLEY

First published 2017

Amberley Publishing
The Hill, Stroud,
Gloucestershire, GL5 4EP

www.amberley-books.com

ISBN  978 1 4456 6316 6 (print)
ISBN  978 1 4456 6317 3 (ebook)

British Library Cataloguing in Publication Data.
A catalogue record for this book is available from the British Library.

Typeset in 10pt on 13pt Celeste.
Typesetting by Amberley Publishing.
Printed in the UK.

# How to claim your
# £75 Wine Voucher

**Step 1** Redeem at virginwines.co.uk/books75

**Step 2** Now use your **£75 wine voucher**
towards any 12 bottle case of your choice

**WineBank from Virgin Wines** - officially the best way to buy wine in the UK
Spread the cost of buying wine with WineBank. Simply save a chosen amount each month, let Virgin Wines
add 20% interest to give you even greater savings, and receive free express delivery on every case.
No commitment - just a great way to enjoy top quality wine for less.

**Plus, if you don't like a wine, let us know and we'll give you your money back**

★ Trustpilot   Rated 'Excellent'
by over 23,500 customers
★ ★ ★ ★ ★

wines | World of Books

# Contents

# Acknowledgements

The following are acknowledged for their assistance in producing this book: Benjamin Pidgeon who read the draft text, making many useful suggestions, and my ever patient partner Mark Metcalfe, for resolving questions of grammar. Thanks are also due to members of the Daimler & Lanchester Owners' Club forum and others who tolerated and responded so generously to my frequent pestering for information and photographs.

Copyright is individually acknowledged alongside each photograph but I would also like to thank those whose pictures did not get to fit into the space available. If we have inadvertently used copyright material without permission or acknowledgement we apologise and will make the necessary correction at the first opportunity.

Finally, two points should be appreciated by the reader when tackling this volume. Firstly, just as in life the BSA Chairman's wife was known as Lady Docker or simply Norah depending on the context, so it is here. Secondly, though the majority were supplied with some sort of standard body, Daimlers and Lanchesters were primarily produced as a rolling chassis – each type of which was described by a code consisting of two letters (the first being D for Daimler or L for Lanchester) and three numbers. Each chassis type was generally given two codes with an even number indicating right hand drive and the following odd number left hand drive. Thus, DF317 would indicate a left-hand drive Daimler Majestic.

# Daimler and Lanchester Up to 1960

## The Origins of the Daimler Marque

The German engineer Gottlieb Daimler, with his partner Wilhelm Maybach, developed the internal combustion engine which became the foundation stone of the car industry. In 1891 Daimler's company granted patent rights in respect of their engine designs to a twenty-eight-year-old British engineer called Frederick Simms. The company Simms set up to hold those rights went through a number of identity changes, before winding up in the hands of Harry Lawson.

Lawson was a financier with a very mixed reputation. He attracted thousands of investors to his schemes while the financial press openly considered him a rogue. His acquisition of Simms' company and subsequent flotation in January 1896 of the Daimler Motor Company Limited (DMC) was part of a scheme to control the British car industry, such as it was, by buying up all the technical rights and patents that he could lay his hands on. The market for cars in Britain was potentially huge but stifled by laws that effectively prohibited their use on public roads in any useful way. However, as Lawson had anticipated, the Locomotives on Highways Act came into force in November 1896 and effectively made motoring legal.

Car production at the DMC got underway but for many years the firm, whose board of directors included a strictly inactive Gottlieb Daimler, was riven with management disagreements, which at one point threatened to leave the firm with no board of directors at all. Daimler himself resigned in 1898. Almost miraculously the firm managed not to implode and enjoyed a brief period of stability before being taken over by the Birmingham Small Arms Co., better known as BSA.

## The BSA Takeover

BSA was formed in 1861 by the amalgamation of fourteen master gunsmiths who supplied rifles to the British government. Trade fell away through the 1880s, such that BSA had to diversify into bicycle manufacture to keep the factory going, although the gun trade later picked up and remained a central part of their activities. By the early 1900s BSA were

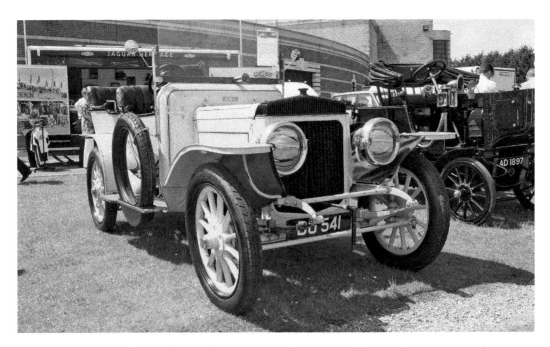

A typical Daimler of the period immediately prior to the First World War. The point to note here is the ribbing on the top of the radiator, which was represented by the fluting along the top of the radiator grilles on later cars. So characteristic was this that until the SP250 of 1958, very few models carried Daimler badging. (Author)

This Lanchester of the early twentieth century is a typical product of its maker; distinctive, technically brilliant and made to the highest standard. (Author)

looking to get into the motor business. Although they manufactured cars under their own name until 1939 and motorcycle production would become and remain a significant activity into the 1960s, BSA needed to acquire an established car maker. Despite their gradually improving profits Daimler really needed the security that being part of a larger combine would bring and so, in 1910, what was by then the Daimler Motor Company (1904) Limited was wound up as part of a £600,000 takeover by BSA. A new company was formed called the Daimler Company Limited, with all shares held by BSA.

## Daimler – War and Peace

Having sorted out their management issues, Daimler was indeed an attractive proposition for BSA. In 1900 the then Prince of Wales had his first experience of motoring on a Daimler; this proved to be the foot in the door they needed to become the warranted supplier of cars to the Royal Household – itself a first step towards establishing themselves as the default supplier to royalty and nobility around the world.

A parallel sales strategy was to employ new technology to give Daimler cars an edge over the competition and, shortly before the BSA takeover, Daimler began fitting all its cars with the Knight sleeve valve engine. In this the normal valve gear was replaced by sleeves sliding up and down within each bore. Apertures in the sleeves and bore were aligned in sequence to form the inlet and exhaust ports. The object was to remove the chief source of noise from an engine, which was the clatter of valves being pushed open and then slamming shut against their seats. The 'Silent Knight' engine was certainly quiet, although the need to lubricate sleeves within the bore meant that oil consumption tended to be high, with most of it heading down the exhaust pipe.

Alongside cars Daimler also developed heavy goods vehicles and buses, which brought them considerable business during the First World War, supplying the army with huge numbers of ambulances, staff cars, mobile workshops, buses, gun tractors and lorries, as well as tank and aircraft engines.

After the war Daimler continued with the production of cars fitted exclusively with sleeve valve engines which culminated in the Double-Six engine of 1926 which was essentially two six cylinder engines joined together on a common crankshaft to create a V12. It was an engine to match the best that anyone could offer. However, as the conventional poppet valve became a quieter and more tolerable device, so sleeve valve engines were phased out during 1934–36. By this time – from 1930 in fact – an equally idiosyncratic device, the pre-selector gearbox (described in Chapter Three), had been introduced across the Daimler range. It brought quick, silent gear changes within reach of the un-gifted amateur driver and remained a distinctive and attractive feature of all Daimler and Lanchester cars for nearly thirty years.

## The Acquisition of Lanchester

Lanchester had been producing cars since 1895 under the direction of Frederick Lanchester, who had a predilection for designing cars from first principles with little reference to what anyone else was doing. This is not usually advisable unless you happen to be a genius. Frederick Lanchester was indeed a genius and the cars he designed were exquisite masterpieces, which was fine for those who bought them, but a matter of continual frustration to Lanchester's board of directors, who were at times reduced to almost pleading with Lanchester to stop refining his latest masterpiece long enough for them to put something into production. Nevertheless, the company was operating well enough until its bank called in its overdraft during the financial crisis of 1931. Daimler, who were attracted by Lanchester's engines as replacements for their now outmoded sleeve valve units, stepped in. Although Frederick Lanchester was retained as a technical consultant, Lanchester cars became little more than badge engineered Daimlers.

## The Second World War

The role of Coventry as host to a substantial chunk of the British car industry, and manufacturing in general, was very well known to the Germans who made it a special concern to flatten as much of the place as they could. Before they got to Coventry the Luftwaffe already had considerable experience of dropping lots of bombs on cities, but even they were sufficiently impressed by their efforts that they invented a new verb – to coventrate – to describe the level of destruction that they achieved during the raids of 1940/41.

Somehow Coventry – and Daimler in particular – managed to keep functioning. Car production ceased for the duration of the war, although some buses were produced in 1942 and Daimler's all-wheel drive scout and armoured cars were produced in large numbers. In peacetime their power units provided the basis for the first generation of Daimler's new car engines.

## Peacetime Reconstruction

In common with most British, and indeed European industry Daimler ended the war in a state of exhaustion. Quite apart from bomb damage, machinery was worn out from years of overuse and the workforce had to be re-established as men slowly returned and displaced the women who had taken their places during the hostilities.

Maintaining a balance of payments surplus, and so restoring international confidence in sterling, was an incredibly high priority for successive post-war British governments. The country's need to gather in export earnings meant that British manufacturers had to qualify for permits to purchase raw materials by selling their products into markets, primarily the USA, for which they had not been intended and were often barely suitable. An additional device was to suppress domestic demand for cars and other durable goods by imposing Purchase Tax and hire purchase restrictions at rates that fluctuated throughout the forties, fifties, and even the 1960s in a series of violent adjustments and over-corrections. To a certain extent the immediate post-war period was no easier for industry than the war years, when at least they knew they had a customer for their output.

## Hooper and Barker

A significant issue for car manufacturers after the war was securing their supply of bodywork. Smaller firms like Daimler were reliant on traditional coachbuilders, who were fast disappearing. Even before the war they had been shutting down for lack of skilled labour and customers. These factors, and the move by car manufacturers from chassis based to monocoque bodies, accelerated the decline of the coachbuilding industry after the war to the extent that, by 1959, it was virtually extinct.

The coachbuilder Hooper, within which Barker was a wholly owned subsidiary, was acquired by BSA in 1940 and became Daimler's in-house supplier of special coachwork. While Barker became no more than a trade name for work produced in Daimler's own workshops, in the few years left to them Hooper maintained a semi-independent existence and provided bodies for not only Daimler but also Rolls-Royce and Bentley. They advertised separately from Daimler and exhibited at international motor shows in their own right. By the end of the decade, however, demand for formal coachwork had almost evaporated and the final straw came when Rolls-Royce announced that the Silver Cloud/S-series replacement would be of monocoque construction. Hooper completed their last body, on a Bentley S2 chassis, in October 1959.

One example of the use of alloy castings in bodies by Daimler, in this case part of the bulkhead of a Daimler DH27. Experience with this technique was one reason why Daimler acquired the coachbuilding firm of Carbodies in 1954. (Author)

# The Departure of Sir Bernard Docker

Sir Bernard Docker virtually inherited the Chairmanship of BSA and Daimler from his father Dudley in the mid-1940s. In 1949 he married Norah Collins who, as Lady Docker, almost immediately began attracting enormous media attention to herself, her husband, and the Daimler company by virtue of her extravagant lifestyle and willingness to share what was on her mind with the world's press.

In the 1930s both the Ariel and Triumph motorcycle companies had been rescued from insolvency by Jack Sangster who then sold them to BSA; Ariel in 1944 and Triumph in 1951. The second purchase involved Sangster joining the BSA board from where he led a successful campaign to have Docker ousted from the Chairmanship in 1956. Sangster and Norah had known each other from childhood, which only added to the Dockers' sense of betrayal. Altogether it was a highly publicised affair, with the board decision having to be ratified by an extraordinary shareholders' meeting after Sir Bernard had taken advertising slots on ITV to put his case to the nation.

When Sangster joined BSA he had brought with him a design team led by Edward Turner who adapted the work he had done on engines for Triumph motorcycles to produce two V8 engines, of 2.5 and 4.5 litres capacity, which were to be used in a new range of cars. Daimler, however, was trapped in an impossible situation, which Docker's departure did nothing to change. Taxation of all sorts was driving away customers for their large cars

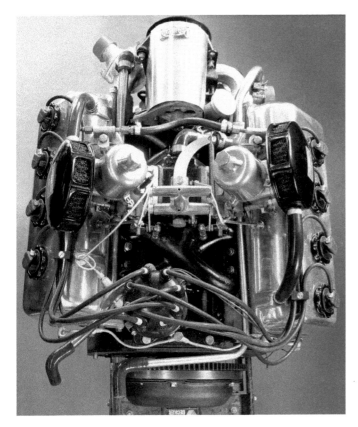

The 2.5 litre V8 engine designed by Edward Turner with all its plumbing in place. The polished dynamo cover bearing a Daimler badge was an unusual but standard fitment when the engine was installed in the SP250. (Nick James)

while they lacked the resources to develop a sufficiently profitable mass production model. The V8 engines were impressive, but the cars they went in merely repeated the policy Daimler had pursued right through the 1950s: one of producing an endlessly changing line-up of models for the same declining customer base. Even the British royal household started buying its cars from Rolls-Royce. It was no consolation to know that comparable marques such as Alvis, Armstrong Siddeley, and even Rolls-Royce were also only hanging on as little more than vanity projects for a wealthy parent company.

By the end of the fifties saloon production had almost halted and even production of the new SP250 sports car was averaging only a couple a week. BSA also had significant problems elsewhere in the group and so when Sir William Lyons expressed interest in purchasing Daimler, he was made extremely welcome. In 1960 Daimler were acquired by Jaguar, the consequences of which are described in Chapter Nineteen. Jack Sangster retired from BSA the following year.

Daimler did not advertise regularly in the motoring press but, when they did, would often place full page colour adverts. Their cars were usually depicted reasonably accurately but, in this instance, the Conquest has been transformed into a far sleeker and more exciting machine than any that ever left the Daimler works. (Jaguar Daimler Heritage Trust)

# 2

# The Dockers

## Dudley Docker – The Father

In 1881 the nineteen-year-old Dudley Docker established Docker Brothers with his brother William as a supplier of industrial varnish and later general paint supplies to the railway industry. This led to him arranging a group of mergers to form the Metropolitan Amalgamated Carriage and Wagon Company, one of the largest employers in the country with over 14,000 employees. Dudley went on to acquire directorships of a number of railway companies and other firms such as W & T Avery Limited (the weighing machine people) and the Midland Bank. In 1906 he became a director of the Birmingham Small Arms Company (BSA) and as Deputy Chairman was instrumental in the acquisition by BSA of Daimler in 1910.

## Sir Bernard Docker – The Son

Dudley's only child, Bernard, was born in 1896 and followed his father, though avoiding Dudley's somewhat aggressive career as a corporate deal maker, into the directorships of several firms including BSA of which he eventually became Chairman. In 1933 he married film actress Jeanne Stuart. Dudley immediately had her privately investigated and dug up enough dirt to get Bernard to agree to divorce her after only a few months of marriage. She went on to become Baroness Jeanne de Rothschild. Bernard went on, in 1949, to marry Norah Collins and if Dudley had lived long enough to see how that turned out (he died in 1944) he would surely have saved himself the cost of all those detectives.

## Lady Norah Docker – The Wife

Born in 1906, Norah was the daughter of Sidney Turner, who ran a car dealership in Birmingham that failed, leaving the family finances in a state of graceful decline. When Norah was sixteen her father succumbed to long-standing depression and committed suicide. At eighteen Norah left home for London where she became a professional dancing partner at the Cafe de Paris. After fourteen years of dancing with a succession of wealthy men, Norah finally succeeded in marrying one; Clement Callingham, head of the wine merchant Henekeys, in 1938. Their son Lance was born within a year, followed in 1943 by a daughter, Felicity, who died at the age of nine months. By the end of 1945 Callingham was also dead.

In 1946 the now forty-year-old Norah married the sixty-nine-year-old Sir William Collins who was chairman of Cerebos Salt. By her own account she married Collins for his money but nevertheless they '...shared a wonderful joy of companionship'. Within two years, however, Collins yielded to long term illness and Norah was now a widow once more.

Inheriting Collins' fortune was a close-run thing, however. Some months before his death he changed his will to leave his fortune to Jack Weedy, his vice-chairman at Cerebos. Norah and Lance would have been cut off with £500 apiece. Fortunately, though not of course for Mr Weedy, Collins changed his will to leave everything to Norah the night he lapsed into a final coma before his death three weeks later.

Not long after Collins' death Norah became reacquainted with a figure from her family's past. Sir Bernard Docker had been a potential suitor of her sister Alma twenty years previously, which suggests that the Turners were not quite so impoverished as many writers are apt to suggest. The big difference between then and 1948 was that Docker's father was now dead and, as powerful as his malignant personality had been in life, even he could not control his son from the grave. Norah and Bernard were married in February 1949, with Norah becoming Lady Docker by virtue of her new husband's knighthood.

## The Dockers – Husband and Wife

There is a persistent myth that Norah spent her youth marrying much richer, much older men. All three husbands were certainly rich but, though Collins was significantly older, Callingham and Docker at thirteen and ten years her senior respectively were not quite from a previous generation. As for the money, Norah's attitude after Collins' death was that she was too rich to need to marry someone poor, which Docker certainly was not. Evidence of his incredible wealth was the *Shemara* – for decades the largest private motor yacht on Lloyds Register – which he had commissioned from Thorneycroft in 1938.

Norah had not involved herself in any conspicuous way in the business affairs of her previous husbands. Whether the worlds of wine and salt had not excited her interest or the husbands had not lived long enough is uncertain, but in Daimler she found a perfect opportunity to express herself. She was made a director of Daimler's in-house coachbuilder Hooper where she made her most obvious impact directing the design of the annual show cars (*see Chapter Eighteen*). According to her autobiography her influence on the production side was more profound. Her view, which she impressed upon Sir Bernard, was that the royal customers were all very well, but they were not enough to keep the company going. What she felt was needed was a Daimler for the masses, or at least masses of the professional middle class, which eventually appeared in the form of the Conquest range.

A Chairman's wife with 'views' can always be a difficult commodity and Norah's in-your-face personality and appetite for media coverage aroused mixed reactions. Many people saw her as a plain speaking Northerner who took people as she found them, regardless of rank, and who felt that her considerable wealth was nothing to be ashamed of.

Sir Bernard and Lady Docker, with the latter's son Lance Callingham, returning from the French Riviera in May 1958. (Keystone Pictures USA)

Others saw her as a brash unguided missile inclined to explode against anything and anyone that she decided to take exception to. Daimler's directors and, on occasion, the Inland Revenue, were particular targets on account of their objecting to the Dockers' habit of racking up huge bills for anything from cars and dresses to the refurbishment of a Welsh castle, and then charging them up as expenses.

Sir Bernard's first professional setback came at the Midland Bank in 1953 when the chairman asked him to resign his directorship. There had been growing disquiet within the Board concerning the increasingly undignified press coverage of the Dockers' lifestyle. The opportunity to act came when Sir Bernard had been prosecuted for infringing the very strict limits on the movement of foreign currency out of Britain which were in force at the time. The offence was extremely minor – involving spending allowances for the *Shemara*'s thirty crew – but it was excuse enough. Sir Bernard at first refused to go but yielded before the matter could be aired at the forthcoming annual general meeting.

When, in 1956, the BSA board and shareholders followed the example of the Midland Bank and forced Sir Bernard's resignation as Chairman, Norah's complaint of unfairness was reasonable but irrelevant. She was quite right that her husband was not guilty of any unique incompetence. The Board, however, had lost faith in Sir Bernard largely, quite apart from the issue of expenses, because of his unwillingness to rein Norah in as she increasingly became the uncomfortably idiosyncratic face of BSA in general, and Daimler in particular. Quite simply the pair of them had come to be seen as an expensive embarrassment.

After their separation from BSA the Dockers began to fall out of the limelight. They were back in it in 1958 after a peculiar incident in Monaco where they were about to attend the reception held after the christening of Prince Albert, the heir to (and current occupant of) the Monégasque throne. Norah's request to bring her son Lance, whose nineteenth birthday was the same day, had been refused, which so enormously offended her that she mutilated a small Monégasque flag from a restaurant table decoration. This got both her and Sir Bernard banned from Monaco and, by the terms of a treaty with France, the whole of the Cote d'Azur. The incident made headlines in Europe and America but was the last incident of note. The Dockers slipped quietly into retirement with only the occasional story appearing on the theme of their declining fortune. In the mid-sixties they sold the *Shemara* and moved to Jersey to escape the effects of UK tax. Sir Bernard died in 1978 with Norah following suit in 1983.

# 3

# The Pre-Selector Transmission

The manual gearbox, as it originally appeared, was a tricky thing to master. To effect a quiet gear change, without knocking bits of gear teeth off, the driver had to double declutch. This meant changing gear by first selecting neutral, then synchronising the gear wheels using the accelerator, before finally selecting the required gear. People with time for that sort of thing could obtain enormous satisfaction from mastering the crash gearbox as it became known; for everyone else it was an embarrassing nuisance. Daimler's solution was the Wilson pre-selector gearbox, which was fitted in almost every Daimler and Lanchester car from 1930 until it was replaced in the late 1950s by the Borg-Warner automatic gearbox.

The pre-selector, self-changing or Wilson gearbox differed from the manual gearbox by having epicyclic rather than parallel gears. In a conventional gearbox the gears slide in and out of mesh with each other on parallel shafts. In an epicylic box the gears are permanently in mesh.

The Wilson gearbox consists of gear sets which each comprise three planet wheels connected by a carrier and a central sun wheel, all inside an annulus. When the annulus is able to revolve, the sun wheel, which is turned by the engine flywheel, revolves the planet wheels which turn the annulus. The planet wheel carrier, which is connected to the gearbox output shaft, does not move and so no drive is transmitted from a gear set in this condition. When the annulus is held stationary, the planet wheel carrier is forced to revolve around the sun wheel driving the propshaft and thus the car. Locking different combinations of annuli produces the reverse and four forward gears. The annuli are locked by external brake bands that clamp around them – the bands being operated by an engagement pedal – while a cam assembly operated by a selector lever determines which brake band is operated.

A gear change is made by first moving the selector lever on the steering column to the required gear position. This is called pre-selecting the gear because this can take place at any time before the selected gear is needed. The actual engagement of the selected gear is effected using a foot pedal, which is pressed fully down and then released. In common with many British cars of this period, first gear is very low and only used on steep hills. Moving off on the flat in first gear provokes rather violent wheelspin.

The only significant hazard the driver risks is that of achieving what is called a false neutral. This happens when the engagement pedal is not applied with firm decisive strokes, resulting in a loss of drive even though a gear has been selected. The first the driver

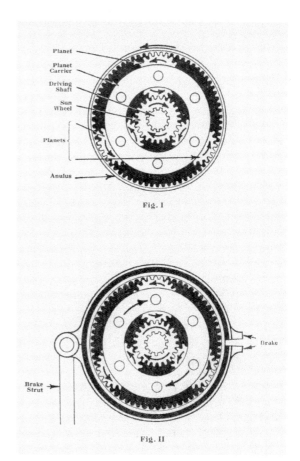

Fig. I

Fig. II

Representations of the construction of an individual gearset within the Wilson gearbox showing how the gears react when the annulus is free to revolve (Fig. 1) and when it is locked by its brake band (Fig. 2). (Jaguar Daimler Heritage Trust)

knows about this is when the engagement pedal does not come back up when it is released or it comes up with great force and much higher than usual. This would be quite alarming to a driver who did not know what was going on. The cure is to press down on the pedal again and release it. This might require quite considerable effort but can and should be done as firmly as necessary, without any fear of breaking the mechanism.

Untutored drivers are inclined to confuse the engagement pedal with the clutch pedal of a manual transmission. It is no such thing and one habit you must never acquire is easing the engagement pedal, as you would a clutch, as this will cause the gearbox brake bands to slip and wear prematurely.

Obviously, with the driver's feet occupied with gear engagement and acceleration, there was a need for some sort of automatic device to substitute for the foot operated clutch. This was where Daimler scored over its rivals, as they were able to obtain a patent on the use of the Wilson gearbox in combination with a fluid flywheel. Unable to use this almost implausibly simple device, other manufacturers using the Wilson gearbox were forced to resort to clutches operated by centrifugal force, electro-magnetism and other such forces of nature. It is the fluid flywheel that gives the Daimler transmission its distinctive sound – a sort of purring whirr if you like it or, according to Lord Montagu who did not, a 'muted banshee wail'.

17

The design of the gear pre-selector lever barely changed from the first in 1930 to the last thirty years later. This one, in a Hooper Empress Mk II of 1953, is slightly unusual in that, because the upper gear ratio is higher than 1:1, its gear position is indicated by 'O' for overdrive instead of being marked 'T' for top. (Bob Frisby)

The fluid flywheel is a hollow flywheel divided vertically into an oil-tight assembly consisting of the driving member (fixed to the engine) and a separate driven member (fixed to the gearbox input shaft). As the driving member is turned, oil held inside the flywheel is flung out towards the rim. Vanes cast inside the driving member direct the oil towards vanes in the driven member, which is thus made to turn and transmit drive from the engine via the gearbox to the rear wheels. This might not sound very effective but, in fact, the fluid flywheel transmits about ninety-seven per cent of the engine's power into the gearbox. The advantage over a conventional clutch is that although the driving member is always trying to drive the driven member, because they are mechanically unconnected the driving member (and thus the engine) won't be prevented from turning when the car and, thereby, the gearbox and driven member are held stationary. Therefore, the car can be brought to a halt and held by the brakes in gear without any risk of stalling the engine. This does, however, mean that the car must not be started in gear (there is no inhibitor switch to prevent this) as the car will immediately move off.

# 4

# Lanchester Ten – LD10

The Lanchester Ten, like so many cars coming into production immediately after the end of the Second World War, was originally intended for launch in 1940 but did not enter production until the very end of 1945. The chassis, designated LD10, featured independent front suspension but was otherwise a continuation of pre-war Daimler design, as was the engine – a four cylinder unit of 1,287cc developing 40 hp. Despite this modest output a top speed of 70 mph was achievable and considered quite adequate by contemporary road testers who also praised the Ten's stability. They found that this, and the engine's smoothness even when pushed hard, made an average driving speed in excess of 40 mph both possible and tolerable over long distances despite the model's marked reluctance to accelerate (0 to 50 mph in 26 seconds for example). The cable and rod operated Girling brakes needed to be applied firmly to give of their best but were sufficiently effective.

Fuel consumption was low with around 35 mpg being possible, with 25 mpg being a realistic average. The launch price of £672 including purchase tax was about the same as an MG Y type and over ten per cent dearer than an Austin A40 Somerset. The LD10 chassis was in production for five years, until 1951 when it was replaced by the LJ200, with output totalling 3,030 cars.

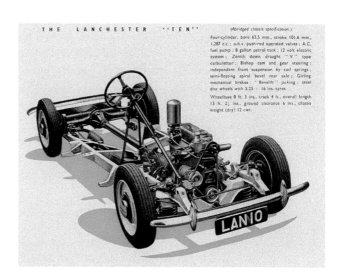

Chassis of the LD10 which was common to all versions. (Jaguar Daimler Heritage Trust)

A Briggs bodied LD10 saloon of 1947. Rear hinged 'suicide' doors were one element of its pre-war styling, although these would still be common on cars into the early fifties. (Steve Glover, Wikimedia Commons)

## Briggs Bodied Saloon

The Ten first appeared with a four door pressed steel body supplied by Briggs of Dagenham. Briggs had a close association with Ford (who would buy them outright in 1953) and this might explain the resemblance between the Lanchester and certain Ford models such as the pre-war Eifel and contemporary V8 Pilot.

In common with many immediate post-war models, the Briggs Ten had a very pre-war look to it. The sit-up-and-beg styling with separate wings and headlamps was a large part of this but the rear hinging doors, opening windscreen, and even the sun roof were features most manufacturers had already dropped. Following the prototype batch of twenty-five cars, a total of 2,426 Briggs-bodied Tens were produced.

## Barker Bodied Saloon

In 1949 the Ten appeared with a new four door body produced by Daimler under the Barker name. This was something of a backward step, being coachbuilt with a wooden frame and aluminium panelling. The motivation for this seems to have been that deliveries from Briggs were becoming unreliable. Although the panelwork ahead of the windscreen did

The coachbuilt body by Barker gives the impression of being a smaller car due to its less upright stance compared to the Briggs model. It is also very much a post war design with the light window frames and generally smoothed out styling, which is typical of new models in the late forties. (Author)

The rear of the Barker design gives a hint of the Lanchester Fourteen and Daimler Conquest which followed. (Author)

not change very much, the new body had a very different overall appearance. There was now no third window behind the rear door, which was itself larger and now hinged from the front. The door window frames were now thin plated channels, rather than being part of the door pressing, as on the Briggs bodies, which gave the car a somewhat airier look, while the back end was very much lower than before.

Only 579 Barker cars were produced, although the number of survivors seems to be about the same for each body type, which in part reflects the susceptibility of the Briggs body to rust, pressed as it was from rather low grade steel.

## Other Bodies

Being a relatively mass produced budget model, the Ten did not attract much in the way of specialist coachwork, although some cars were fitted with individual bodies produced outside the BSA group, such as two-door Drophead Coupes by Abbott and Wentworth. Two vans are known to have been constructed by Hooper.

# 5

# Lanchester Fourteen / Leda – LJ200/201

Within a few years the styling of the Lanchester Ten was looking old-fashioned and a replacement was relatively quick in coming. This was the Lanchester Fourteen, which was launched at the 1950 London Motor Show.

The new car was based on the LJ200/201 chassis, which was fitted with a new 60 hp four cylinder 1,968cc engine – practically fifty per cent bigger than the LD10 engine in terms of power and cubic capacity. The main chassis alteration concerned the introduction of torsion bar front suspension that offered simplicity and reliability, which would be essential for a model that was intended to have relatively mass-market appeal.

The Fourteen's launch price was £1,391 – a considerable step-up from the £1,170 being charged for the last of the LD10s. Two years later this had risen to just over £1,533 tax

LJ series chassis, common to both the Lanchester Fourteen and Leda. The layout of side members linked in the middle by cross members arranged as an 'X' was common to most Daimler chassis. (Jaguar Daimler Heritage Trust)

inclusive, which reflects both UK price inflation and government tax policy. The LJ series chassis continued in production for three years, until 1953, when it was given a substantial makeover, renamed the DJ series, and re-launched as the basis of the Daimler Conquest range. This meant the effective end of Lanchester production after fifty-five years, although under BSA ownership, since 1931, the name had been little more than a marketing label.

## Lanchester Fourteen

The Ford-like styling of the LD10 was replaced by a much more up-to-date body design, which owed something to the contemporary Humber Hawk. The Fourteen was launched with what was described at the time as a coachbuilt body. This was, and remains, a source

Lanchester Fourteen. The roof mounted aerial is a factory fitted item. In the early fifties even mid-range cars rarely made provision for a radio. The Lanchester even provided for the speaker to be fitted under the headlining and came with a string threaded down the windscreen pillar to pull the speaker wires through with. (Andrew Bone, Wikimedia Commons)

Rear view of the Fourteen showing its resemblance in this area to the preceding Barker bodied Lanchester LD10. (Author)

of some confusion, since what was meant by this was not a body of metal panelling over a traditional wood frame, but a pressed steel body that incorporated cast aluminium structural elements. The most significant of these were castings which formed the framing for the door apertures, including the sills. Their use was evidenced by the pop rivets which attached them to the adjacent steel panels.

## Lanchester Leda

In 1952 the all-steel Leda was launched, which used an identical body to that of the Fourteen except that the alloy castings were replaced by steel pressings. Superficially the Leda is only distinguishable from the Fourteen by its name, which appears on the enamel strip below the bonnet mascot. The two models were sold in tandem, with the Leda (initially at any rate) being available for export sales only, whilst the Fourteen was restricted to the

Dashboard of a Lanchester Fourteen. The gauge cluster includes a speedometer, ammeter, fuel and water temperature gauges but, in common with all other BSA built cars, no engine oil pressure gauge, merely a warning light. (Author)

Bonnet mascot representing the face of the goddess Leda fitted to all Lanchester Fourteen and Leda models. The enamel strip is blank on the former and carries the model name on the latter, which is the only way of telling the models apart from the outside. (Author)

24

UK market; certainly the Leda was eventually sold in the UK and it is most probable that the Fourteen was kept in production simply to use up the last of Daimler's stock of alloy body frames. The Leda sold for £885 (pre-tax) against £985 for the Fourteen.

And who was Leda, whose head was modelled in the rather neat bonnet motif? She was the wife of a Spartan king who was visited by Zeus, appearing in the form of a swan. The result of this visit, full details of which have no place in a respectable publication of this sort, was that she laid two golden eggs which hatched to produce a son and a daughter, the latter being Helen of Troy. No obvious connection with mid-range motor cars but perhaps customers liked the idea of buying their car from a classically educated manufacturer.

## Lanchester DHC and Roadster

Apart from the four door saloon the only other potential variant to emerge from Daimler's workshops was the two door 'De Ville Convertible'. This had very similar styling to the saloon and was fitted with a three position hood – i.e. closed, de ville, and open. In the de ville position the portion of hood over the front seats was furled by hand back to a rail in line with the rear edge of the doors. Raising and lowering the rear portion of the hood was achieved by an electro-hydraulic mechanism. Although this model was officially announced very soon after the saloon was launched (with a list price of £1,634 including tax), it only existed as a prototype and failed to enter production until after the launch of the Conquest, when it did so as a variant of that model.

There were also plans for a sports car, to be called the Lanchester Roadster, which did not proceed to the prototype stage before the LJ chassis had been superseded by the DJ chassis, which provided the basis for what eventually entered production as the Daimler Conquest Roadster.

## Lanchester Dauphin – LJ252

Appearing right at the end of LJ production, the Dauphin was described as a sports saloon – the sports bit doubtless being a reference to its being based on what was, in effect, a Daimler Conquest chassis, although it was given a Lanchester designation, LJ252. The body, built around alloy framing, was a two door Empress-style saloon by Hooper.

Though it might seem a bit of an oddball there was a precedent in the form of the Triumph Mayflower, which, with sales of 35,000 in three years, had demonstrated that a market for a small saloon with very formal styling certainly existed. The fact that only two Dauphins were produced was mainly due to a tax inclusive price of £4,010, which would have bought you nearly eight (admittedly not nearly so well trimmed) Mayflowers or nearly four Ledas.

# 6

# Lanchester Sprite – LM150/151

In the mid-fifties with Conquest production coming to an end, Daimler faced being left without anything close to a mass production model. The Sprite was an attempt, two attempts in fact, to produce a Conquest replacement and begin the transition from chassis mounted to monocoque bodies.

The first phase of the Sprite development project produced a four door saloon which was exhibited at the 1954 London Motor Show. This car sported a combined bonnet and front wings assembly, which hinged upwards as a single unit to give access to the four cylinder 1,622cc engine. Running gear resembled that of the Conquest with torsion bar front suspension, although the brakes were fully hydraulic and there was no self-lubricating system fitted.

The car's chief novelty was that it was fitted with the Hobbs Mecha-Matic gearbox and would have been the smallest car on the market with an automatic transmission. This was important because fully automatic gearboxes were becoming increasingly fashionable ('two pedal control' would be the buzz phrase in the motoring press during 1956) and, for a couple of years at least, seemed likely to become ubiquitous. In the late thirties Daimler had toyed with automating the Wilson gearbox using electric servos but by the mid-fifties they had no choice but to offer fully automatic transmission on their larger models. However, being able to offer it in the small car market, where it would have no immediate competition, was an especially attractive prospect.

Valiantly attempting to compete with the mighty Borg-Warner corporation of America, the Hobbs gearbox was one of a number of indigenous devices doing the rounds of the British car industry at this time. BSA was so concerned about the need to secure a source of automatic transmissions for the whole of the Daimler range that they took shares in the Hobbs company and financed further development work. The Mecha-Matic utilised hydraulically operated brakes and clutches to control a series of epicyclic gear sets.

Then something very odd happened.

Visitors to the 1955 London Motor Show, expecting to see last year's Sprite now finally a production reality, would have found cause to rein in their expectations. The Sprite was indeed on display, except that it had now been remodelled so that it resembled a Conquest with window frames that were part of the door pressing and a boot that anticipated the rear end of the Majestic. The bonnet was now separate from the front wings whilst the running gear was essentially unchanged. What it was that possessed Daimler to present

Phase 2 Lanchester Sprite showing how the front end retained the styling of the Conquest. (Jaguar Daimler Heritage Trust)

a new model that looked almost identical to the one they were about to discontinue is unknown and defies speculation. Nevertheless, this model – known informally as the phase two Sprite – was seriously marketed with brochures and even a handbook being produced. In the end only three prototypes were made before the whole project was cancelled by the new Chairman Jack Sangster. It was felt that the Sprite would never make a profit at the price it would have to be sold at and the attempt to create a Conquest replacement then shifted to the DN250.

After BSA had sold their shares in Hobbs Transmission Ltd to Westinghouse the Mecha-Matic achieved some success as an optional fitment in smaller-engined versions of the Mk 1 Ford Cortina. Otherwise, apart from a single example of a phase 2 car, the only aspect of the project to survive was the name; rights to which were acquired by the British Motor Corporation for their small Austin-Healey sports car, which appeared in 1958.

# 7

# Daimler DB18 and Consort Range

## 70 hp DB18

Having spent the Second World War producing armoured vehicles and other military hardware, Daimler resumed car production at the end of hostilities with a model that was an update of a pre-war design. The DB18 was launched in September 1945 and was essentially a reworking of the 1939 Daimler 15.

Daimler's war work was used to some effect in that the engine, derived from that used in their pre-war Dolphin rally cars, had been developed further for its use in the Daimler Scout, a light all-terrain vehicle produced for the British army. The six cylinder 2,522cc unit,

This DB18 caught mid-restoration shows off the independent front suspension. (Author)

fitted with a single 1½ ft SU carburettor, gave a maximum 70 hp with fuel consumption around 22 mpg.

The chassis was fitted with independent front suspension (IFS), which should not be taken for granted. For example Alvis, who had pioneered IFS, had been forced to launch the contemporary TA14 with an almost vintage beam axle front suspension. Cable operated brakes and a built in jacking system by DWS were rather more obviously pre-war touches but the automatic chassis lubrication to the suspension and steering joints was a useful

*Above*: Daimler DB18 showing how, typically for the period, the running board has disappeared as designs moved towards full width styling. (Trevor Johnsson)

*Right*: From this angle the DB18, still featuring a flat fronted radiator grille, could be a pre-war model. Note the flat edges either side of the bonnet, which were a feature of Daimler designs from the 1930s until the Majestic of 1958. (David Alderson)

KCD 580

DB18 dashboard. The two large knobs on the top rail are the windscreen wiper switches whilst the crank handle in the middle operates the top hinged opening windscreen. The aluminium panel is a modern addition. (Trevor Johnsson)

feature. Another traditional component was the worm drive rear axle, which Daimlers had used since before the First World War, although it was the last model to have this.

The DB18 first appeared with a standard six-light saloon body by Mulliners of Birmingham. The internal structure was a combination of steel and laminated wood. The provision of an opening windscreen, sunshine roof, and separate headlamps was rather old-fashioned, but it was at least modern enough to lack running boards.

An alternative standard body on the same chassis was a two door drophead coupe. These were mostly made by Barker but a similar looking (but £85 dearer) alternative was made by Tickford of Newport Pagnell.

The cost of the saloon was £1,340 including tax whilst the Barker DHC was £1,425 including tax. Both models were discontinued in 1950 with the home market launch of the Consort.

## 85 hp DB18 Special Sports Series

Introduced in autumn 1948 as a higher performance version of the DB18 chassis, production of the Special Sports overlapped with both the DB18 and the Consort. Peak power was increased to 85 hp at 4,200 rpm through engine modifications which included the fitment of twin SU carburettors.

The most numerous and best known application of this chassis was underpinning the Barker Special Sports. This was a drophead coupe, which offered accommodation for three with the single rear seat facing sideways. The body design, constructed in aluminium over an ash frame, owed nothing to the saloon, which was a model of solid understatement, whilst the Special Sports was positively voluptuous. To complete the effect it usually appeared in two-tone colour schemes that would have given the average DB18 owner heart failure. As a herald of fifties brash glamour it was certainly ahead of the crowd and customers lined up at the rate of two a week with over 390 sold before the introduction of the DF chassis based replacement in 1952. A factory approved permanent fixed head conversion was marketed by Appleyard of Leeds Ltd and found a handful of customers.

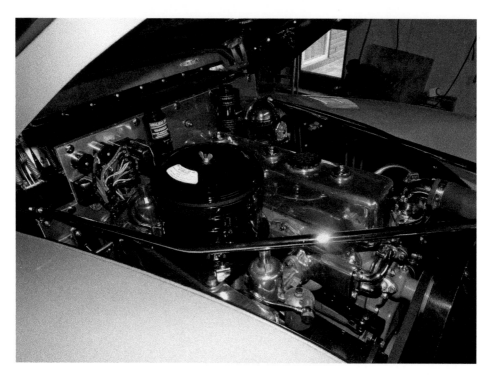

This DB18 Special Sports engine is rather better presented than the standard finish of green paint over all metal surfaces. It does show, however, the extensive use of alloy castings for engine components. (Terry Gorman)

The DB18 Special Sports is almost invariably given this two-tone paint treatment, though usually with metallic colours. The crease immediately behind the front wheel arch can look like a dent but is actually a styling feature intended to make the wing look less slab sided. (Author)

The DB18 Special Sports carried a wide selection of gauges by AC, which were used in almost every other Daimler model, though with black faces from 1956, until the Majestic of 1958. (Author)

DB18 Empress in front of the old railway station in Boise, Idaho. The front indicators are a later addition to replace the semaphore trafficators (just visible in the door pillar). When indicating a turn the illuminated trafficator arm on the appropriate side flips out. These were considered unsatisfactory even in the 1950s. (Bob Frisby)

Hooper used the Special Series chassis as the basis for the first of their Empress model, launched in 1950. Despite its appearance the DB18 Empress saloon was not a big car and preserving the proportions of a low-built limousine on such a small chassis resulted in something only 6 feet 3 inches tall outside and very much less inside. Nevertheless it attracted ninety-seven customers, which was no mean feat at a price of £3,450, or just over twice the price of a Consort.

Hooper produced a further nine specials including six dropheads, one of which went to HM King George VI, and a one-off two door touring car in 1951 for Lady Docker.

## 70 hp Consort

The Consort saloon was introduced in September 1949, initially for export only. It can be thought of as an updated DB18, although the update was considerable and no mere cosmetic exercise. The chassis, still designated DB18, was mechanically updated with a bevel rather than worm drive axle and Girling hydro-mechanical brakes.

The more obvious, though still subtle, difference between the old and new models was the body design. The structure was now all steel; a shortage of skilled body makers meant that timber-framed construction was no longer economic on anything large scale. Steel bodies are also far easier to produce with consistent quality.

The new standard saloon body was very similar to that of the DB18 apart from a reshaped rear, faired in headlamps, and a more rounded sloping grille. The anachronistic opening windscreen and sunshine roof of the previous model did not appear on the new car. The DB18 drophead coupe was replaced by a Consort drophead by Barker which, as with the saloon, resembled the earlier model but with the new headlamp and grille arrangement.

The cost of the saloon in 1951 was £1,623 including tax, rising at one point to over £2,000. The Consort ran for three years until it was replaced in 1953 by the Conquest.

The Consort was largely unchanged in appearance from the DB18 except for the adoption of a more rounded radiator grille and headlamps mounted directly into the front wings. (Author)

33

# 8

# The Daimler Straight Eight – DE36

Post-war Daimler car production had commenced with the DB18 but was quickly followed in 1946 by the launch of two models which catered for altogether more exalted markets. They were the eight cylinder DE36 and its six cylinder companion the DE27. The DE36 was aimed firmly at the very highest end of the car market. 'Possibly 'fabulous' is the most embracing term for a car that is considerably the most expensive in the world... /and/ ...has the largest wheelbase and biggest body space of any European car', as *The Motor* put it in December 1947.

The chassis conformed to usual Daimler practice with widely spaced side members with substantial cross bracing. The outer members tapered in sharply at the scuttle to accommodate the independent front suspension whilst, at the rear, they swept up and over the underslung axle that broke with Daimler tradition by having a hypoid rather than Lanchester worm drive. In order to produce a low flat floor the drive line was lowered by inclining the engine down at the rear by five degrees with a similar inclination of the rear axle.

The length of the DE36 chassis gave coachbuilders, in this case Hooper, scope to create some of the most elegant and well proportioned bodywork ever made. (Jaguar Daimler Heritage Trust)

The engine, the last straight eight in production by the end of its life, was based on the six cylinder engine developed by Daimler during the war for their armoured car. The 5,460 cc unit produced 150 hp, which on the road translated to a typical top speed of about 85 mph, and fuel consumption in the region of 10 mpg; not that running costs were of immediate concern to owners of a car costing almost as much as five DB18s. At launch the total cost of a factory limousine was £6,410 7s 1d, which was split almost evenly between chassis, body, and purchase tax.

A wheelbase of 12 ft 3 in and overall length of over 18 ft gave coachbuilders the opportunity to create some of the largest and most spacious limousines ever built. It is difficult to be precise about production numbers. A total of 216 chassis numbers were set aside for use on DE36s, of which 145 have been confirmed as definitely constructed. Hooper built a total of 114 bodies for DE36 chassis (mostly standard limousines), whilst Windover and Freestone & Webb produced a pair of designs each which together accounted for another eighteen cars. The remainder were almost all one-off specials.

Easily the most glamorous of the DE36s were the 'Green Goddess' convertibles. The name was not one given by Daimler but was used in a review of the first such car when it was displayed at the London Motor Show in 1948. With a total price tag of £7,001 it was the most expensive car in the world and at 20 ft long the owner of this and the six very similar cars that followed certainly got a lot for their money.

The DE36 was catalogued until 1953 although the production timetable is not as straightforward as it is for the smaller cars. For example, the first DE36 chassis was

Although the coachbuilding industry was rapidly closing down, Hooper did not have things all to themselves. Freestone & Webb constructed this touring limousine in 1950 for the Bishop of Leeds. (Davocano, Wikimedia Commons)

built in 1947 but the completed car was not delivered until early 1949. An examination of such build and registration records as exists indicates that completed chassis sat for years in some cases, either at Daimler or with the coachbuilder, before being completed and registered.

Often overlooked is the role of 'the carriage trade' in maintaining the market for the larger chassis, in this case DE36, which customers for limousines alone were increasingly unable to support. Hearses also provided vital trade for a number of specialised constructors. (John Nash)

# 9

# Twenty-Seven Horsepower Range – DE27/DC27/DH27

## DE27

Although the DE27 was a smaller version of the DE36, which it closely resembled, it was by any standard a very large car. It differed from its larger stablemate by having a wheelbase of 11 ft 6 in – some nine inches shorter; however, most of the standard bodies from Hooper, Windover, and Freestone & Webb were designed to fit either chassis. The main difference was the engine – a straight six of 4,095cc producing 110 hp. This engine was based on that used in the armoured car Daimler had produced during the Second World War.

*The chassis illustrated is the " Twenty-Seven." The " Straight-Eight " and " Twenty-Seven " are identical in design but have eight- and six-cylinder engines respectively. Both accommodate coachwork of identical style and size.*

DE27 chassis showing how the engine was inclined downwards at the back to give a lower driveline and floor. The device below the front of the engine is one of three scissor jacks attached to the chassis, the other two by the rear wheels. (Jaguar Daimler Heritage Trust)

Typical example of limousine coachwork on a DE27 chassis. (Author)

A total of 203 chassis numbers were allocated for the DE27 and certainly over a hundred cars were constructed. The in-house coachbuilder Hooper built thirty-three limousines in two main styles, as well as about nine limousines under the Barker name. Barkers themselves produced a nine-seater limousine specifically aimed at the private hire trade with a total price of £4,341.

Windover produced twenty-six limousines and twenty-five saloons – the only owner driver cars built on the DE27 chassis. Freestone & Webb produced a dozen cars whilst Charlesworth also made several cars, although the number is not known. Vanden Plas produced two identical four-door convertibles, ordered by the Indian cricketer 'Ranji', which were fitted with Lanchester radiator grilles.

## DC27 – Ambulance

Undoubtedly the most distinctive of all 1950s Daimlers were the ambulances of 1948/53. The chassis itself was very similar to the DE27 except that the engine was not only inclined down at the back, but also positioned at a diagonal so the rear end pointed slightly to the nearside. This was done to facilitate the connection with the rear axle differential, which was located on the left, rather than centrally, thereby producing a flat central loading area. The chassis itself was especially large with a wheelbase of 12 ft 6 in.

These vehicles were expensive but highly regarded by crews for their ride quality. This was partly due to the smooth gear changes made possible by the pre-selector transmission but also the sheet of cement cast into the floor, which gave the ambulance an especially low centre of gravity. It also contributed to braking efficiency, which could be frighteningly modest.

Ambulance bodies were constructed by Barker and Hooper. These can easily be distinguished by the chrome strip down the side; two for Hooper and one for Barker.

The unusual offset driveline of the DC27 ambulance chassis is immediately apparent. (Jaguar Daimler Heritage Trust)

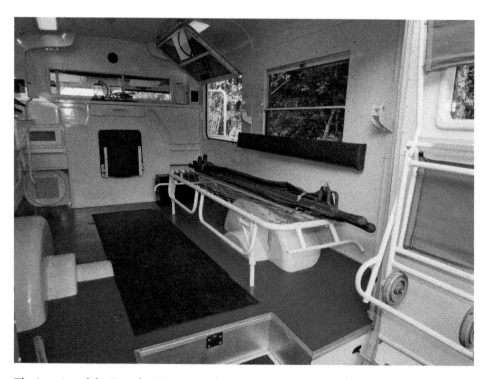

The interior of the Daimler DC27 ambulance was especially spacious and uncluttered. The upward hinged window on the right was an escape route if an accident prevented an exit through the doors. (Author)

*Left*: The driver's compartment of the Daimler ambulance was rather cramped in order to provide as much space in the working area as possible. (Author)

*Below*: The Daimler ambulance was the largest in regular production as is apparent in this view. (Author)

Although 500 chassis numbers were allocated, it would seem that no more than half a dozen were produced in any one year so that total production was about thirty. This might explain the curious case of the DH27.

## DH27

The DH27 is unusual among Daimlers of this period in that its designation actually stands for something. The DH is a reference to Daimler Hire Limited, which was established before the war by the purchase of a hire car firm run by Harrods. By the 1950s the firm had been bought by the Hertz company but was still using Daimlers for its limousine fleet. The seven seater limousine bodies were constructed by Hooper and featured electric divisions and large 'sight-seeing' windows. The rolling chassis was a combination of DC27 chassis frame and DE27 running gear.

All of the DH27s were supplied in one single batch of sixty cars over the first half of 1951; this was an unprecedented (and unrepeated) sales achievement for any model of Daimler car at this time. One must suspect that production of the DC27 had not matched Daimler's ambitions and that some sort of special deal was done with Daimler Hire in order to shift an overstock of ambulance chassis frames.

As has already been said, the Twenty Sevens and Straight-Eights were in large measure very similar in appearance – how then can you tell the different types apart? The ambulance is obviously a distinct model but the passenger cars almost all follow the following 'rules'; DE36s had two spare wheels mounted in the front wings and chromed vents along the bonnet sides, DH27s have side mounted spare wheels like the DE36 but no bonnet vents, and the DE27s have bonnet vents but no external spare wheel.

The very substantial construction of the larger Daimler chassis is apparent in this view of a DH27 rolling chassis. The hole in the cross member on the left is where the driveshaft would pass through on a DC27 ambulance. (Author)

# 10

# Three Litre Range – DF300/301/302/303)

In 1951 Daimler introduced the first in a range of models based on the same 3 litre engined chassis. The engine itself was essentially a 90 hp six cylinder version of the four cylinder unit used in the Lanchester Fourteen which had been announced the previous year. To a great extent the 3 litre models followed a pattern established by the DB18 range; i.e. saloon, convertible, and Hooper Empress formal saloon, all based on the same chassis with a higher performance engine for the latter two models.

Production levels were extremely low; this was not because of any shortcomings in the cars themselves, but rather one of the sudden crippling rises in Purchase Tax which plagued the British car industry for much of the 1950s. Only seven Regency saloons and thirty-three DF302/3 chassis were produced. Among the latter were a few specials; a couple of two door Empresses, a single fixed head version of the convertible, and possibly the 1953 Earls Court show car *Silver Flash*. Cars on nine prototype chassis included one similar to *Silver Flash* completed in 1952.

## 90 hp DF300/301 Regency Saloon

The first 3 litre model to appear was the Regency four door saloon. The thoroughly up-to-date body, incorporating cast alloy a-posts and constructed by Daimler under the

The first Regency saloon captured the style of the Jaguar Mk VII without the excitement. A very rare model then and almost extinct now. (Jaguar Daimler Heritage Trust)

Barker name, followed the lines of the DB18 Special Sports introduced two years earlier. Basic price was £1,500 with a total UK price of £2,334 16s 8d including tax.

The chassis was fitted with independent front suspension using coil springs supplemented by telescopic dampers. The rear suspension used conventional semi-elliptic springs. Girling hydro-mechanical brakes and a thermal automatic chassis lubrication system were fitted in common with the Consort, from which the 3 litre's chassis was in large part derived.

## 100 hp DF302/303 Special Series Chassis, Convertible Coupe and Hooper Empress Mk II

A year after the launch of the Regency the Convertible Coupe was unveiled at the 1952 Paris Motor Show. This model was fitted with a more powerful 100 hp version of the saloon engine and priced at £2,661 10s 0d including tax.

This Convertible Coupe very closely resembled the DB18 Special Sports which was still in production. The chief visible differences between the two models were that the new Convertible had a forward-facing rear seat for two passengers rather than the DB18 model's sideways-facing single seat. Also, the doors were hinged at the front with the semaphore trafficator housed in the door itself rather than in the rear wing as on the Special Sports, which had rear-hinged 'suicide' doors. Less obvious features of the new model were power operation for the hood and windows.

Following the pattern of the DB18 range, from 1952 the DF302/303 chassis was offered with formal saloon coachwork in the form of the Empress Mk II, which was distinguishable from its predecessor by having an additional side window behind the rear door – i.e. was a six rather than four light design. Coinciding with a general tax-induced slump in car sales, this version did not sell more than thirty-three examples.

The 3 litre Special Sports greatly resembled its DB18 predecessor, although the forward-hinged doors are an easy recognition point, as is the very unusual positioning of the trafficators in the doors. (Jaguar Daimler Heritage Trust)

The Hooper Empress Mk II had some resemblance to its Regency saloon counterpart. The main change at the front from the DB18 based predecessor was the fitting of inbuilt foglights in place of air intake grilles. (Bob Frisby)

The extra length of the 3 litre chassis over that of the DB18 was shown by the addition of the window behind the rear door. (Bob Frisby)

Show cars aside there was never anything overdone about Daimler interiors with the simplicity of style belying the quality of the workmanship. The picnic tables in the back of the front seats became almost an essential for luxury cars of the fifties and sixties. They were, however, one of those accessories that people always think are going to be more useful than they actually are. (Bob Frisby)

# 11

# The 3.5 Litre Range – DF304 to 311 and 314

In 1954, after three years' production, the 3 litre range was given a radical overhaul with a new engine of 3.5 litres created by increasing the bore of the 3 litre unit, which boosted net power from 90 to 107 hp. This was a very necessary upgrade because, whilst chassis changes, apart from the engine, were minimal, the new models' bodywork had become larger and heavier. So much so that, even with the extra power, performance with this engine only just matched that of the 75 hp Conquest.

## Regency Mk 2 – DF304/5

The Regency Mk 2 saloon was five inches longer and two inches lower than its predecessor. This adjustment gave it rather sleeker proportions and a roomier interior which featured picnic tables in the back of the front seats. The frontal appearance was updated by moving

The Regency 2 brought the original 3 litre version visually into line with the rest of the Daimler range by moving the headlamps out to the edge of the front wings. (Jaguar Daimler Heritage Trust)

DAIMLER REGENCY. This big new Daimler is available with either a 3½-litre or 4½-litre engine and is notable for the interior spaciousness and luxurious furnishings of its five-six seater pressed steel body and for its comprehensive equipment which includes matched fog and road lamps.

the headlights out to the front wings rather than being positioned between them and the radiator grille. The alloy castings in the body of the previous model were replaced at some point with steel pressings. Basic price including tax was around £2,324.

## Hooper Empress Mk IIa and Mk III – DF306/7/8

Now based on the 3.5 litre DF306/307 chassis, but with bodywork unchanged, the Empress was now designated Mk IIA. Net power was raised – by 14 hp compared to the Mk II – to 114 hp by using an aluminium head and raising the compression ratio. With the introduction of the One-O-Four in 1955, the Empress was moved to the 130 hp Sportsman DF308 chassis – again with no noticeable changes to the body design, but re-designated Mk III.

## Sportsman – DF308/309

The Barker three-seat convertible, which had been the sports tourer of the 3 litre range, was replaced by a totally different model called the Regency Sportsman. This closely resembled the Regency saloon except that it featured a larger wrap-around rear window, the rear wheels were covered by deep spats, and the boot was angled much more sharply with the

The Regency Sportsman was identical to the standard saloon as far back as the rear doors. The bonnet opens along the centre line, which does not provide the best engine bay access. (Author)

The distinctive design of the Regency Sportsman is most obvious from the rear. The heavily spatted rear wheels and sloping boot resemble those of Jaguar's III, although the fins rather spoil the effect. (Author)

rear lights carried on small fins. The chief attraction, however, was the engine, which had been further modified to produce 130 hp. In common with the Empress, the Sportsman was fitted with a gearbox in which top gear was effectively an overdrive gear (as opposed to direct drive as on the saloon). The tax inclusive price of £2,650 represented quite a considerable premium over the saloon model.

## One-O-Four – DF310/311/314

In 1955, a year after its introduction, the Regency Mk 2 was re-launched as the One-O-Four. The name reflected the top speed of this new model, which featured a yet further uprated engine producing 137 hp. The DF310/311 chassis had been modified to stiffen the body structure and incorporated vacuum servo assisted brakes. There were numerous detail changes to the interior and exterior fittings. Due to the fluctuating nature of Purchase Tax, which had so damaged sales of the 3-litre range, the price varied during the model's production life between £2,260 and £2,828.

An interesting addition to the range was the One-O-Four Lady's Model. This was a standard One-O-Four but with the addition of, in the words of the brochure, 'a galaxy of especially feminine features'. Some were functional refinements such as electric windows and a more accessible clock adjustment knob, apparently inspired by Lady Docker who wanted one that would be less likely to cause chipped nail varnish. The dashboard boasted

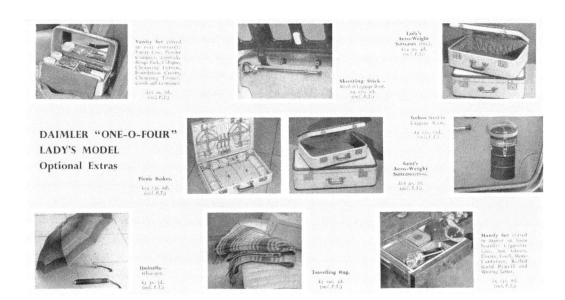

DAIMLER "ONE-O-FOUR"
LADY'S MODEL
Optional Extras

The extra fittings in the Lady's Model version of the One-O-Four were made available to individual order. None of them were cheap but the travelling rug seems especially expensive. (Jaguar Daimler Heritage Trust)

labelled and varnish friendly switchgear and a polished alloy instrument panel of a style that was and remained unique to this model.

Most of the extras were simple accessories that spoke volumes about the sort of woman Daimler thought they could draw into their showrooms. The rugs and suitcases and even the umbrella and fitted road map were quite conventional. More unusual was the fitted case of Max Factor cosmetics, while the dashboard featured a drawer containing a gold pencil, notepad, sunglasses, and cigarette case. Completing Daimler's vision of the lady owner's lifestyle was a picnic case, shooting stick, and Thermos ice box. Very few cars were sold with the full package of accessories, with Daimler quickly offering them as extra cost options.

## Final Developments

With the introduction of the One-O-Four the other two models were up-rated by moving up a chassis. The Empress was now offered on the Sportsman chassis while the Sportsman was now based on that of the One-O-Four. Additionally, some models (*described in Chapter Thirteen*) were also offered with an alternative 4.5 litre engine.

In 1956 the British car market was in the full grip of a mania for what was popularly called 'two pedal control' or fully automatic transmission. Daimler responded by offering Borg Warner transmission across its range, including the One-O-Four, which in this form was designated DF314. One of these chassis was used as the basis for the Daimler Continental produced by Hooper as an answer to the Bentley Continental, with which it was hoped to compete as a fast, well-appointed touring car. In the event, the car produced for the 1956 London Motor Show remained a one-off.

# 12

# Daimler Conquest Range – DJ250 to 257 and 260/261

## 75 hp Chassis – DJ250/251 – Conquest Saloon

At the end of 1952, BSA were producing two medium range models. The Daimler DB18/ Consort series had been in production for seven years and was ready for replacement by something more up-to-date. The Lanchester Fourteen/Leda had only been in production for three years and was much more up-to-date, especially as regards styling. The Lanchester brand, however, had become rather meaningless and the decision was made to discontinue the Leda and recycle it to produce a replacement for the Consort at a price somewhere between the two. The Conquest range of cars was launched in May 1953 at the obviously marketing-inspired price of £1,066 plus tax.

Compared to the four cylinder two litre engined Lanchester Leda, the most obvious differences for the Conquest model were the six cylinder 2.5 litre engine and Daimler grille.

The Conquest chassis frame was of quite lightweight construction compared to those of the larger models though of similar design. The only significant change from that of the Lanchester Leda, apart from on some early cars, was from side jacking points to ones built into the ends of the side members. (Author)

*Above*: This dashboard is in a very early Mark 2 saloon. The burr walnut is Mark 2-style veneer, but the dashboard style is still Mark 1. (Author)

*Left*: The Mark 1 Conquest was fitted with built in foglamps, which are often cracked. The handbook warns against using them when the car is stationary because the glass cannot withstand the heat from the bulb. Not one of Lucas' better designs.

The interior was also upgraded; especially noticeable was the change from the Fourteen's rather utilitarian Bakelite-framed instrument cluster to an impressive array of AC instruments of the same type used in the larger Daimlers. The pressed steel bodyshell (produced in Oxford by Fisher Ludlow, then owned by Morris Motors) was carried over largely unchanged from the Leda.

The Conquest's engine was initially in the form of a 75 hp unit equipped with a single Zenith carburettor and a cast-iron cylinder head. This was only fitted to the Conquest Saloon types DJ250/251; all other models were fitted with the Conquest Century unit, which developed 100 hp and was fitted with two SU carburettors and an alloy head.

## 100 hp Chassis – DJ252/253 – Convertible Coupe

The Conquest Convertible Coupe was a revival of the convertible version of the Lanchester Fourteen, which had been announced in 1951 but was never actually produced. The all-steel two-door convertible body was designed and constructed by Carbodies – a Coventry based coachbuilder, which was taken over by BSA in June 1954 – chiefly because of their experience in the use of alloy castings in coachbuilt bodies and ability to undertake short run production jobs. The body design closely resembled that of the saloon, as did the interior; although, curiously, unlike every other Conquest model fitted with the 100 hp engine, the instrumentation did not include a rev counter.

The Conquest Drophead Coupe shared a great deal of its panelwork with the saloon. It was only produced with the Mark 1-style front end. (Author)

The hood was a patented Carbodies design used on similar convertible conversions they had undertaken for Rootes, Ford, and Austin. This was a three position type, which, in addition to fully closed and open, offered a coupe de ville position where the material over the front seats was furled back with the rear part of the hood still erect. This rear part was folded using electro-pneumatically operated rams, which not only raised the hood up and down but also tipped the rear seat backrest back and forth in sequence to allow the hood to move in and out of its compartment behind the rear seat. Only 234 were built before the model was nominally replaced by the New Drophead Coupe sports car.

## 100 hp Chassis – DJ254/255 – Sports Models

In order to build the national economy back up after the expense of the Second World War, the British government had promoted the earning of foreign currency by a policy of linking permission for industry to purchase raw materials with export sales. The problem for the car industry was that this really meant sales into the USA, which was persistently indifferent to British mass production models. Sports cars – now that was a different matter, as MG had been showing since 1947 with their T-series Midgets. It therefore made complete sense for Daimler to use the Conquest chassis as the basis for a new sports car. The fact that they had never produced such a thing before was beside the point; after all, the name of Jaguar had meant little to Americans until they started clambering over each other to buy the XK120 of 1948.

An additional benefit of a Conquest sports car was that it would draw attention to the 100 hp engine that Daimler were about to fit in the Conquest Century saloon. So with everything making perfect sense they got to work and created the Daimler Conquest Roadster.

The Regency style extended to the rear of the Roadster where the fins resembled those of the Sportsman. This particular car was the second prototype, which probably appeared on the Carbodies stand at the 1954 Earls Court Motor Show. (Jaguar Daimler Heritage Trust)

The Roadster was a neat attractive design, though with more of a Regency look about the front wings than Conquest. (Author)

Some design work had already been done on what would have been a Lanchester Fourteen Roadster and this enabled the creation of a prototype in a matter of weeks prior to exhibition at the London Motor Show of 1954. In appearance it resembled, in so far as it resembled anything, the contemporary MGA, albeit with a Daimler grille up front and prominent fins carrying the lights at the rear. Vents in the rear wings hinted that here was a car so fast it had to have holes cut in the body to keep the brakes ventilated. In fact the vents led straight into boot, serving no purpose at all apart from cooling the spare wheel, and were not repeated on production cars. Contrary to many published descriptions the body did not contain any alloy framing, but was constructed as a rather crude steel frame attached to saloon floor panels. Even the front inner wings and grille were modified from saloon pressings. The body frame was clad with an aluminium skin with steel bonnet, boot lid, and doors.

In terms of performance the Roadster sat quite respectably between the MGA and the Austin Healey 100-6. It was not an unattractive looking thing and the handling was everything it needed to be; and yet sales were so poor that one has to conclude that whatever it was that Daimler were thinking of it certainly was not opening up a new market in the New World or indeed anywhere else. The majority of Roadsters were produced over the course of 1954 with a few stragglers built up in the middle of 1955, taking the total, including prototypes, to fifty-two, which was rather less than one week's production of the Triumph TR2.

The immediate issue was price, which was within £100 of the Jaguar XK140 – to which it was in no way an equivalent. It was a £900 car selling for nearly £1,700. It is hard to

53

The Roadster body frame was a very simple affair, built on a standard saloon floor pan. The bars across the doorways have been welded in to maintain the correct door apertures while the body is lifted from the chassis during restoration. (Author)

see where that price came from except that body production entailed a great deal of hand work. In some respects this was to overcome the sort of mistakes people make when they design things in a rush. For example the rear inner wings seem to have been designed by someone who was not in communication with whoever was making the outer skins, so the inner wings on each car had to be dented to allow the outer skin to fit over the top.

Given the way it was designed, the Roadster's body simply could not be constructed in worthwhile numbers with the likelihood of any significant profit. Yet, after a pause in production, Daimler repeated the exercise. This time they spent a year producing a revamped model now styled the Conquest New Drophead Coupe, its launch coinciding with the cessation of the four-seater Conquest Convertible Coupe. Reflecting the general trend of increasing comfort in sports cars this new model was essentially the Roadster with wind up windows, lockable doors and a heater. It also boasted a sideways-facing third seat in the rear in the style of the DB18 Special Sports. With a price that had crept up to nearly £2,000, the new model was hardly any more successful than the Roadster had been, with sixty-seven cars produced during 1956/57.

An attempt to expand the range with a rather nice fixed head version of the New Drophead Coupe came to nothing with one prototype built and an awful lot of brochures printed.

The dashboard of the Conquest sports models was a very simple affair, especially so for Daimler, although the modifications carried out to Sir Norman Wisdom's car by Hooper included an Empress-style veneered dashboard. This is a New Drophead Coupe as evidenced by the controls for the heater which the Roadster did not have. (Beat Weibel)

The New Drophead Coupe differed from the Roadster, chiefly in having wind-up door windows and exterior door handles. (Beat Weibel)

The fixed head version of the New Drophead Coupe was a serious proposal and a lot of brochures, from which this illustration is taken, were printed, but only one car was ever made. (Jaguar Daimler Heritage Trust)

## 100 hp Chassis – DJ256/257 – Century Saloon

The Conquest Century saloon was announced as an additional model in spring 1954. In addition to having the same 100 hp engine as the Roadster, the Century was distinguished by the addition of a rev counter, chromed front and rear screen trim, decorative chrome trim on the bootlid, a rear seat positioned four inches further back, and even two suitcases. Top speed at 90 mph was an improvement of about 10 mph over the 75 hp model.

Absent from this Mark 2 Conquest are the fog and driving lamps, which were mounted on the overriders. The built-in foglamps were replaced by grilles, one of which served the intake for a larger heater. The MGA type front lights are a later modification that provides a neat way of installing indicators. (Gillian Barry)

56

The Conquest was one of Daimler's better balanced designs. In this view it is apparent how much cabin length was given over to the rear seat passengers. (Gillian Barry)

The Mark 2 Conquest dashboard used the same instruments as in the preceding model, albeit with black rather than cream faces, which were standardised across the Daimler range. This car is a moderately rare DJ260 automatic, which is apparent from the gear selector lever. (Gillian Barry)

There were a number of small variations in items such as seat covers and steering wheels but the saloons were substantially unchanged until autumn 1955 when they were upgraded to produce the Conquest 2 and Conquest Century 2 with no change in chassis designation. These revised models featured bigger freestanding foglights, a much improved heater, a revised dashboard with black-faced instruments replacing the earlier cream dials, and burr walnut veneer replacing the straight grain veneer of the earlier cars. This upgrade was phased in with, for example, many early Mark 2 cars being fitted with the earlier style dashboard, albeit with the walnut veneering.

# 100 hp Chassis – DJ260/261 – Automatic Transmission

In 1956, by the end of which the Century saloon was the only Conquest model left in production, Daimler began to succumb to the contemporary enthusiasm for automatic transmission. A Borg-Warner automatic gearbox was offered as an alternative to the pre-selector box before replacing it entirely in September 1957. The Conquest Century saloon was discontinued in January 1958. By this time the company was sliding towards its eventual takeover by Jaguar in 1960 and a replacement, if such it can be called, did not appear until the launch of the (Jaguar Mk 2 based) Daimler 2.5 litre V8 in October 1962.

## Special Bodied Cars

There was no routine use of the Conquest chassis for coachbuilt specials, although about ten saloon based estates were built. These included six for use as camera cars by the television news company ITN. The smooth gear changes made possible by the pre-selector transmission apparently made it an especially stable platform for mobile filming.

Hooper did produce a handful of Empress-type bodies, including two examples of what was marketed as the Lanchester Dauphin. Given the chassis designation LJ250, this was a two-door Empress-type saloon built by Hooper in 1954 on the Century chassis. Although this was a listed model, with a price more than double that of the standard saloon, it is not surprising that it failed to find a market.

Effectively a miniature Empress, Hooper manged to retain reasonably graceful proportions on the comparatively small Conquest chassis whilst providing realistic headroom for the occupants. (Geoff Douglas)

The side view shows how well Hooper managed to avoid the rather dumpy look that tends to afflict formal bodywork on a small chassis. (Geoff Douglas)

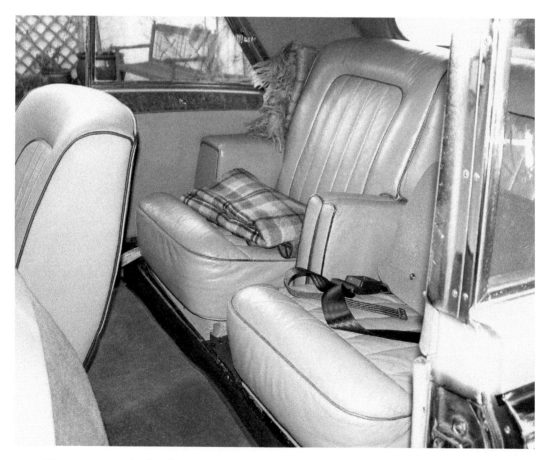

These rear seats look to be supremely comfortable. In fact they are apparently rather awkward to get in and out of and generally inferior to the standard saloon item to sit on. (Geoff Douglas)

# 13

# The 4.5 Litre Range – DF400/401/402/403 and DK400/401

A large chassis suitable for the limousine and associated carriage trade market had always been a vital element in the Daimler model range even if by the early 1950s the smaller models were numerically and commercially more significant. In the immediate post-war period this requirement was covered by the DE27 and DE36 chassis. Production of these ceased in 1951 and 1953 respectively to make way in late 1954 for the DK400/1 chassis. This was powered by a 4.5 litre engine, which Daimler had been trying to use in a number of existing models with very mixed results, few of them satisfactory.

## 127 hp Chassis – DF400/401

The engine was a larger bore version of the 107 hp 3.5 litre unit with a capacity of 4,617cc, initially producing 127 hp. The gear ratios were amended to match the new engine's capabilities and the direct gear was moved down from top to third, while top became an overdrive gear. Apart from this the only significant difference from the 3.5 litre equivalents was the use of a fully hydraulic (rather than hydro-mechanical) braking system incorporating a vacuum booster. The resulting combination was sold in the form of Regency Mk 2 and Sportsman saloons priced at £2,777 and £3,103 including tax respectively.

## 167 hp Chassis – DF402/403

For 1956 the 3.5 and 4.5 litre engines were uprated and the latter now produced 167 hp. In this form the chassis was designated DF402/403 and again offered in the form of Regency Mk 2 and Sportsman saloons. However, this level of power was too much for the gearbox and most if not all of these cars were recalled and fitted with 3.5 litre engines.

Total released production of the DF400/1/2/3 series was only around two dozen cars from late 1954 up to 1958 when the range was replaced, along with the 3.5 litre models, by the Majestic.

# 167 hp Chassis – DK400/401

The DK400/401 chassis was essentially the DF saloon chassis with a longer wheelbase and wider track to accommodate limousine bodywork. Its only real point of interest is that it was the last new chassis from Daimler to be fitted with a pre-selector gearbox.

DK400/401s fall into two main groups; those with chassis numbers starting 92, which were all, with one exception, fitted with coachbuilt bodies by Hooper, and those with chassis numbers starting 96, which were the standard Daimler limousine. The only difference between them mechanically was that automatic chassis lubrication was deleted on the 96 series chassis and replaced by conventional grease nipples.

The 92 series comprised twenty-five chassis, of which nine were sold to customers outside the BSA group for building up as hearses. The remainder, with the exception of a prototype standard limousine by Carbodies, were fitted with bodies by Hooper; eight cars in one of two designs, including the last of the Hooper Empress series, and the other six as one-offs. Many of these Hooper cars were produced at fabulous cost for exalted customers such as the Queen Mother, the King of Afghanistan, HH Sultan of Johore, the Governor of Sierra Leone, and the Lord Mayor of Cardiff. They also included two 'Docker Daimlers'; *Stardust* of 1955 and *Golden Zebra* of 1956. With only two exceptions these Hooper-bodied cars had a front wing line that rose up over the headlamps to form a sort of hood – a feature that would reappear in less-pronounced form on the Jaguar XJ6 of 1968.

An example of what was effectively the Hooper Empress Mk IV, though not marketed as such. (John Nash)

An alternative design from Hooper, which is basically their Empress design with a different treatment at the rear wheel. This car featured in their press advertising. (Jaguar Daimler Heritage Trust)

The 96 series comprised 106 chassis, which were mostly used for a new limousine model aimed chiefly at the private hire trade. The genesis of this model was a one-off built on a chassis from the 92 series by Hooper and exhibited as the Regina at the Earls Court Motor Show in 1954. Although it was described as being a new standard model, the car that eventually went into production differed in many respects, especially at the rear.

Another prototype was also produced on a 92 series chassis by Carbodies. This was a very unsatisfactory design, which arose from them being given the impossible task of producing a limousine in the style of the One-O-Four saloon. It was exhibited on Carbodies' stand at the Earls Court Motor Show of 1955 and again it was suggested that this was the first example of a new model. Thankfully it remained unique but that contemporary suggestion has misled later writers into believing that Carbodies were responsible for the car that did eventually enter production in early 1957. In fact, the bodies were produced by The Abbey Panel & Sheet Metal Company – a Coventry firm outside the BSA group who produced panelwork for a number of firms such as, a few years later, bonnets for the E-type Jaguar and bodies for the Ford GT40.

Who styled the production model and how such a large quantity of bodies came to be constructed outside the BSA group is an intriguing mystery. Whatever the truth is, the standard limousine, with some hearses that shared the same front end panelwork, was not an especially elegant design but doubtless lent an air of awesome solemnity at the funerals that were its natural environment. Indeed, DK400s from the Daimler Hire fleet made up the tail-end of the motor cortege at the funeral of Winston Churchill. The potential for sales to private customers was reflected in the availability from late 1957 of the DK400B, which

This is the prototype for a standard DK400 limousine which Carbodies were requested to construct but which was not repeated. The building on the right is the fire station at Daimler's Radford factory, the site of which is now a housing estate. The fire station has survived and today houses the Tiny Teddies Nursery. (Jaguar Daimler Heritage Trust)

The standard DK400 limousine, looking like an extremely large taxi, which is essentially what it was. (Jaguar Daimler Heritage Trust)

was fitted with an electric division, two occasional seats, and a radio console in the rear compartment as opposed to the sliding division, and three occasional seats of what now became the DK400A.

Prices were in line with the model's position as one of the biggest luxury cars in production. The standard limousine cost £4,195 (DK400A) and £4,315 (DK400B). The coachbuilt cars obviously varied but the standard Hooper limousine retailed at £6,213. The DK400/401 was available until it was replaced by the Majestic Major limousine in 1961.

The plain functional dashboard of the DK400 standard limousine was like that of the Conquest Century Mk 1 on a larger scale although, oddly, there was no lockable glovebox. (Author)

Interior of the DK400B aimed at the private owner, as opposed to the hire car market and funeral directors. It was common practice for the rear seats in private cars to be trimmed in cloth, whereas the front seats and the rear seats of cars sold for hire use were usually trimmed in harder wearing and more easily cleaned leather. (Jaguar Daimler Heritage Trust)

# 14

# Daimler Majestic Range

## Majestic – DF 316/317 and DF318/319

By the beginning of 1958 the Daimler range was a mix of models being produced in ever-declining numbers. The best-selling model had been the 2.5 litre Conquest range, but that was now five years old and about to be discontinued, whilst the 3.5 and 4.5 litre One-O-Four models were looking very old fashioned compared to the competition.

Launched in July 1958, the running gear of the new model was based on the outgoing 3.5 litre One-O-Four. The engine was enlarged to 3,794cc, which, along with a modified cylinder head, raised the power output to 147 hp. However, although the chassis retained the overall design of the previous model, there were several features which marked the Majestic out as a break with traditional Daimler practice.

The Majestic looked very much more modern that the cars it replaced, although the front end drew heavily on the outgoing One-O-Four. The sidelights were the same as the front pilot light on some contemporary Triumph motorbikes, a product made by another BSA subsidiary. (Author)

Most immediately noticeable was that the only transmission option was the Borg-Warner automatic. For the first time in decades Daimler were offering a new model without at least the option of a pre-selector transmission. Other new features included four wheel disc brakes – probably a first on a British saloon car – and power steering as an optional extra. The automatic chassis lubrication system that had featured on all Daimlers since the 1930s was absent; also missing was the flat ledge running along the bonnet sides, which had also been a longstanding Daimler feature.

The body was noticeably more modern looking than previous models, although some front end panels had been carried over from the One-O-Four. The radiator had been lowered by a couple of inches and the front wing line ended at the front doors with the rear body being more smooth-sided. This not only looked more up-to-date, but also released more elbow room inside. The interior fittings were in the same style as previous models although, curiously perhaps, there was no rev counter.

Bodies for this and the related Majestic Major models were supplied by Carbodies, for whom the job was an ongoing nightmare. The root of the problem was that a shortage of money meant that the body was essentially a variation of the One-O-Four design. Steel press tooling for the new panels was out of the question on grounds of cost. Carbodies, however, had been pioneers in the use of a zinc-based alloy called Kirksite, which was cheaper to cast than steel. Tools made from this metal did not have the working life of steel but that would not have been a huge issue for what was never planned to be a high production model. The problem was that Daimler could not even afford to finance new tooling in Kirksite.

The Majestic dashboard, curiously, did not feature a tachometer and still no oil pressure gauge. The switches were the same as those used on some rather humbler BMC cars but dressed up with chromed surrounds and labelled. (Author)

The solution – if it could be dignified as such – was to produce a female mould in the shape of each new panel. Into each of these moulds was inverted the corresponding One-O-Four steel press tool and the gap between them filled with molten Kirksite, which was encouraged to bond to the steel tools by bolts screwed into the face of the tooling. The result, in the words of Carbodies historian Bill Munro was '...in effect cast steel tools with lumps of Kirksite stuck to them, and the body panels pressed from these tools were appalling.' Once body production was underway a pit had to be dug alongside the production line. This put men at a comfortable position while applying the considerable amounts of lead necessary on each bodyshell to give the lower part of the panels the correct shape.

The chassis designations DF316/317 were changed in 1960 to DF318/319 to coincide with a number of alterations to such items as the rear axle ratio, water pump bearing and rear brakes. The price of the Majestic varied between a launch price of £2,495 and £2,352 during 1962, the last year of production.

## Majestic Major Saloon – DQ450/451

At the end of the 1950s Daimler was attempting to breathe fresh life into a brand which had become something of an anachronism. The culmination of this programme was the

The Majestic Major differed from its smaller engined sibling with an enlarged boot but from this angle the most obvious identifier is the 'flying D' ornament, which was at that time the closest thing to a mascot ever fitted to a standard production Daimler. (George Zdanko)

launch at the 1959 Earls Court show of the Majestic Major. This model, which entered production in November 1960, was substantially based on the Majestic, whose 3.8 litre straight six engine was replaced by an all-new 220 hp 4,561cc V8.

The new power unit, closely resembling the 2.5 litre version which had already appeared in the SP250, attracted considerable praise, not only for producing more power than any Daimler had seen before, but especially its remarkable smoothness. Until now Daimlers had been powered by engines of modest horsepower and unremarkable design, but this was the time when Britain was entering what was becoming known as the 'motorway age'; motorists were at last able to expect cars to cover long distances at high speed, a role for which this new 120 mph car was clearly suited. It was by quite a margin the fastest car in its class; the Rolls-Royce Silver Cloud II came close with a 0–60 mph time about a second longer than the Major's 9.6 seconds, but with a much lower top speed of just over 100 mph.

Though six inches longer than the Majestic, the Major was visually almost identical. Twin exhaust pipes and front air intakes displaying a V motif were almost the only distinguishing features. The dashboard instrumentation featured black rather than chrome-plated bezels and included a rev counter. The interior trim was in the customary Daimler style and included picnic tables in the back of the front seating. An important optional extra was power steering, which was standardised in 1964. Priced at just over £2,500, sales commenced in late 1960 and totalled 1,180 cars before production ended in 1968.

Compared to the Majestic dashboard, the Major's instrument panel was enlarged to incorporate a tachometer and the instrument and switch surrounds were black rather than chromed. (Author)

# Majestic Major Limousine – DR450/451

In 1961 a limousine version of the Majestic Major was introduced to replace the DK400. A first prototype by Carbodies was rejected in favour of a neater design by Motor Panels, which incorporated the extra length behind rather than between the rear doors. Compared to the saloon, the rear compartment was lengthened by two feet and featured an internal division, as well as two folding seats ahead of the rear bench seat. Performance was hardly reduced compared to the saloon, making it even more of a class leader in this respect.

Apart from the Rolls-Royce Phantom V, at about three times the price the only comparable vehicle on the market was the already ageing Vanden Plas 4 litre Limousine. The lack of competition reflected the almost non-existent market for formal limousines outside of the carriage trade. Priced around £3,300, total sales of 864 equated to less than half a dozen a week.

The Majestic Major range had entered production just as Daimler transferred from the BSA group into Jaguar ownership. They provided Jaguar with prestige models, which maintained the credibility of the Daimler brand long enough for it to be re-invented as a top level variant of Jaguar models. They were eventually replaced in 1968 by the DS420 limousine. Although this replacement was based on the Jaguar 420G, it was still a uniquely Daimler model, until it too ceased production in 1992.

At nearly nineteen feet long the Majestic Major Limousine was two and a half feet longer than the saloon, making it by quite a margin the longest British car in anything like regular production. (Author)

# 15

# Daimler Dynamic – DN250

The DN250, or Daimler Dynamic as it might have been called, was an attempt to address two separate issues facing Daimler in 1958. The first was that when production of the Conquest saloon ended at the end of 1957, Daimler were left with nothing in its range smaller than the 3.8 litre Majestic. Development of the Lanchester Sprite was the most serious attempt to provide a replacement but, quite apart from its own shortcomings, it did not tackle Daimler's other pressing issue, which was that they were developing a 2.5 litre V8 engine that had no home to go to apart from the SP250 sports car, which was never, in anyone's estimation, going to sell in sufficient numbers to justify the cost of bringing the new engine into production.

There was no settled design for the DN250 concept and this sketch from early in the project shows an attempt to create a Daimler identity with minimal changes to the Cresta's body panels. Later styling models used a traditional Daimler grille with an increasingly modified body design.

The idea behind the DN250 project was to largely skip over the process of designing a new car by inserting the small V8 engine into a Daimlerised version of another manufacturer's existing production model. This would not only avoid a lot of development cost but also neatly sidestep the need to design a monocoque bodyshell – a task for which Daimler lacked any experience. Accordingly, in 1959 a styling prototype was put together using Vauxhall Cresta body panels, whilst a complete Cresta was bought by Daimler, fitted with the new engine and used for road testing.

The arguably rather flashy and certainly relatively downmarket Cresta was hardly an ideal starting point, not that there were many realistic alternatives for Daimler to choose from, and the intention was always to modify the bodywork to give it its own more dignified appearance. As the project developed, however, the proposed amendments became more substantial, thus increasingly undermining the whole point of the thing.

The underlying concept, however, was perfectly sound and after the acquisition of Daimler by Jaguar, it was revived in 1962 in the form of the Daimler 2.5 litre V8, which was essentially a re-badged Jaguar Mk 2 powered by the Daimler V8 engine. Being based on something more obviously suitable than the Vauxhall there was less of a need to make expensive engineering and styling changes, thus keeping costs down to a sensible level.

# 16

# Daimler Dart – SP250

By early 1958 work was underway on the development of the first fundamentally new Daimler engines in decades. These were intended to form the basis of a fresh range of cars that would effectively almost re-launch the Daimler brand that was widely seen as the preserve of funeral directors and mayors. The engines would both be V8s, in itself a quite radical move – the first application of which would be in 2.5 litre form in a sports car, which would give the new engine a high profile launch in much the same way that Jaguar had used the XK120 to debut their XK engines ten years earlier. However it was hoped that the new model would be a significant revenue earner in its own right, chiefly in the North American market.

The 2.5 litre Daimler V8 engine has an almost agricultural appearance especially when surrounded by the pipes and cables of its essential services, like a sort of automotive Centre Georges Pompidou. (John Burrough)

The SP250 has an almost conventional shape for a sports car of the late fifties; almost but not quite. It is as though the designer has embraced surrealism to produce the automotive equivalent of Dali's melting watches. (Author)

The car was launched at the New York Motor Show in April 1958. The intended model name 'Dart' was swiftly dropped when the American manufacturer Dodge claimed prior rights and the model was thereafter marketed under its chassis designation 'SP250'.

The design was a real curate's egg; good in parts and less so in others. The engine was impressive as were the four wheel disc brakes. The glassfibre body was a curious design incorporating elements of Triumph TR3 at the back, MGA at the front, and other bits of more uncertain parentage. Glass fibre was only just beginning to make an appearance in the car industry but mainly for non-stress bearing components, such as the cooling fan surround and gearbox tunnel on the Alvis TD21. Its use for bodywork on production cars was confined to Lotus and the makers of certain bubblecars for whom, as for Daimler, it brought two major advantages; low weight and low tooling costs. Whatever the merits of the unusual body styling, such a curvaceous design in steel would have been an economic impossibility.

Unfortunately, the chassis frame was a virtual copy of that used for the TR3, which was fine except that it had been designed for use with a steel bodyshell. What Lotus understood, but Daimler perhaps did not, was that a glass fibre body contributes very little to chassis rigidity in the way that a steel shell does. Using the TR chassis design without modification resulted in body flex that afflicted the model to some extent throughout its production life. Early cars were prone to doors popping open while cornering and the B-series model introduced in April 1961 incorporated body strengthening that significantly addressed this issue. The C-series model sold from April 1963 incorporated as standard such fittings as a heater, which had previously been optional extras.

Stripped bare, the bodyshell (complete with optional hardtop) begins to look a little less odd and its 'facial' resemblance to the contemporary MGA becomes more obvious. (Nick James)

Certainly the SP250's least striking aspect and looking rather like a Triumph TR3 with fins, and quite modest ones compared to the Sunbeam Alpine being produced at the same time. (John Burrough)

This restored chassis shows how little there is to hold the SP250's fibreglass body in shape. It is no flimsier than, say, the chassis of the Conquest Roadster but that had a steel floor pan to stiffen things up ... (Nick James)

The UK launch price was £1,395 including tax, which placed it alongside such competitors as the Austin Healey 100-6 and Jaguar XK140. The SP250 was, however, a distinct offering, which partly explains why Jaguar felt able to continue production until 1964 – more than three years after their takeover of Daimler.

At the Earls Court show of 1959 Hooper exhibited on an SP250 chassis what was probably the last body they produced. Crafted in metal it looked something like a Farina-styled Austin A40 with the nose of an MGA. This strange confection was later written off, although Hooper's chief designer did later construct half a dozen similar cars in fibreglass.

Much more worthwhile was a design study called SX250 exhibited at the 1962 Earls Court show by David Ogle Associates. This had been created at the behest of Boris Forter, a joint MD of the British Helena Rubinstein company, and then used by Reliant as the basis for the body design of their Scimitar SE4.

At about the same time Jaguar made a fairly serious study of how the car could be developed to continue production on a larger scale. The result of this was a prototype that addressed a number of issues that were felt to have been holding the car back from greater acceptance; these included better suspension and steering and wholly new and much more conventionally styled bodywork. Given that these changes would have brought the car into closer competition with the E-type it is not surprising that this model never entered production.

# 17

# Daimler V8-250

When Daimler were taken over by Jaguar in 1960 there was no small saloon in their range and the new 2.5 litre V8 engine was only being used in the low production SP250. It was no great surprise, therefore, when in 1962 this was mated to the successful Jaguar Mark Two to produce the Daimler 2.5 V8. Dropping in a genuine Daimler power unit and making a few subtle changes to the trim somehow transformed the bank robbers' chariot into a dignified carriage. Jaguar had entered a previously unavailable market with little impact on sales of the host model.

Almost incredibly the 3.8 litre Mark Two was the fastest production saloon in the world when it was launched in 1959 so it is not surprising that the suspension and four wheel disc brakes were pretty much state of the art. With the Daimler's V8 putting out 140 hp (rather than the 3.8 litre's 220 hp) the new car would be working well within the car's abilities. In keeping with its image, initially only a Borg Warner automatic gearbox was fitted. In 1967 a manual box could be specified, which was quite a novelty to most customers who would have had only the dimmest memory (if any at all) of the last Daimler model to have been fitted with such a thing. Less obvious but as revolutionary was that this was the first production Daimler with a monocoque body.

Externally the Daimler was identifiable by a fluted variant of the Jaguar grille that resembled the one fitted to *Silver Flash*, which Hooper had exhibited at Earls Court in 1953. Internally the Daimler had a split bench seat rather than the separate seats fitted to Jaguar versions.

Sales of the Daimler were very worthwhile and indeed it was the most successful Daimler model up to that time. The final sales total was almost 18,000 cars in seven years, which comfortably exceeded even the sales of the entire Conquest range – a shade over 9,700 in five years. The model on which it was based, however, had first appeared in 1955 and by the mid-sixties was getting rather long in the tooth. Jaguar were fully occupied with what would become the XJ series, which meant that by the mid-sixties they had a range that was running out of steam. The Jaguar compact range was kept going by price reductions made possible by various cost savings such as Ambla rather than leather trim. The Daimler was largely immune to these measures (it even kept its fog lamps as standard fittings) but was renamed in August 1967 the Daimler V8 250. Production finally ended in July 1969 when the Daimler Sovereign version of the new Jaguar XJ6 became available.

Jaguar styling came almost exclusively from the mind of its Managing Director, Sir William Lyons, who made few mistakes, and the Mk 2 Jaguar, on which the Daimler 2.5 V8 was based, was certainly not one of them. Note the 'flying D' motif repeated from the Majestic Major. (John Burrough)

If anything the mild facelift that produced the Daimler V8 250 improved matters by substituting a slimline bumper for the sculpted steel girder of the previous model. (John Burrough)

# 18

# The Docker Daimlers

Until the end of the fifties there were two ways of buying a Daimler; either as a complete car or as a rolling chassis, which would then be fitted with a body by a separate coachbuilding firm. Daimler's parent company BSA had acquired the coachbuilder Hooper along with its subsidiary Barker in 1940. Whilst the latter became little more than a marketing label for certain standard models, Hooper continued to supply bodies to special order and through the fifties produced, under their chief designer Osmond Rivers, some of the most elegant coachwork ever created, which was mounted on not only Daimler but also a great many Rolls-Royce and Bentley chassis.

Until their industry effectively died out at the end of the 1950s, coachbuilders exhibited alongside motor manufacturers at the world's motor shows, and their stands featured cars designed to show off what they could produce given the right budget. What made Hooper's show cars so successful in attracting publicity to themselves and the Daimler brand in general was good design and superb craftsmanship, but mostly a hefty dose of what we would now call bling, courtesy of the Chairman's wife.

Following her marriage to Sir Bernard Docker, Chairman of the BSA group, which owned Daimler and Hooper, Lady Norah Docker was appointed to the board of Hooper. She had a very real and highly publicised involvement in the design of Hooper's show cars of 1951 to 1955, which were known from the outset as Docker Daimlers.

The question of whether the considerable publicity the cars brought Daimler was worth the amount they were costing became a matter of bitter dispute among the directors of BSA and contributed to Sir Bernard losing the Chairmanship. Certainly other manufacturers thought the concept worth copying, such as BMC with their Austin Healey 100-6 show car of 1958, which appeared with gold-plated brightwork, elephant ivory steering wheel, and seats upholstered with white mink inserts.

## 1948 – The *Green Goddess*

Dubbed by the press the *Green Goddess*, this twenty-foot-long five-seater convertible was built on a Daimler DE36 chassis and, with a price of £7,001, was the most expensive car in the world. As the centrepiece of Hooper's stand at the first post-war London Motor Show in 1948, with subsequent appearances at the New York and Paris shows, she performed

The original *Green Goddess* still under construction in Hooper's workshop. (Jaguar Daimler Heritage Trust)

the serious task of sending out a vital message. Britain was exhausted by six years of all-out war and practically bankrupt, but Daimler and Hooper had survived and were more capable than ever of producing the most magnificent cars in the world. In this she was very successful. Apart from generating considerable press coverage for what was, after all, a very small car maker, she inspired orders for five more bodies in the same style on the Daimler DE36 chassis, as well as at least another two on Rolls-Royce Silver Cloud chassis.

Having been created a year before Norah's marriage to Sir Bernard Docker and her entry into Daimler's affairs, the *Green Goddess* is not a Docker Daimler. In fact Norah was not at all keen on the car, which she described as being 'as heavy as a tank and almost uncontrollable'. For the next two years things were quiet on the Hooper show stands. In retrospect, however, the *Green Goddess* was a hint of what was to come.

## 1951 – The *Gold Car*

The first of the Docker Daimlers and described by *The Motor* as 'the most magnificent motor car in the world'; also known as the *Golden Daimler*, she was built on a Daimler DE36 chassis and carried a quite conventional, albeit extremely elegant, limousine body. A novel feature of the body design was the mounting of the headlamps behind Perspex panels, which blended with the shape of the wings. The finish and trimmings, however, were more unusual.

All the external brightwork from the grille and bumpers to the door locks were gold plated. For some reason Lady Docker felt obliged to provide the rather unconvincing explanation that this was because of a shortage of chromium. One can only assume that at this early stage of her activities she was still unsure of what she could get past the BSA board. The coachwork was finished in black with the side panels below the waistline decorated with thousands of tiny hand painted gold stars. Even the instruments had gold markings on a black background.

The rear compartment was trimmed with specially commissioned hand-woven golden silk and featured a glass roof panel with an electrically operated shutter. The central division contained picnic fittings by Cartier whilst the boot held fitted suitcases in black crocodile. At some point the car had a complete re-trim with the upholstery being recovered with a different design of silk cloth and the wooden door cappings and window trim replaced by crocodile skin. Total cost was somewhere in the region of £8,500 – about the cost of eight 1.5 litre Jaguars.

The car was used privately by the Dockers, as were all the show cars, but was also exhibited in France, America, and Australia. Whilst in France for the opening of Daimler's Paris showroom it was borrowed for the shooting of a scene in the film *Gentlemen Marry Brunettes*. The Dockers naturally accompanied the car for the showroom opening. Not so natural was Norah's wardrobe of dresses by her favourite designer Mme Fanny Chiberta. These included an all-gold dress, another in black with gold stars, a mink stole, and more besides – all of them charged up as business expenses, a move that impressed neither the Inland Revenue nor the board of BSA.

## 1952 – *Blue Clover*

Again based on a Daimler DE36 chassis, this car carried a fixed head coupe body. The front wing treatment with twin headlights inset behind Perspex panels was similar to that of the *Gold Car*.

The glazing was a particular feature with the windscreen and rear quarterlights being made from Triplex heat-reflecting glass, double-glazed electrically operated side windows,

Where the previous year's show car had stars, 1952's *Blue Clover* had four-leafed clovers. Several thousand of them and all the work of one man. (Saratoga88 – Wikimedia Commons)

and a glazed panel above the front seats, which could be closed off by an internal blind. The already huge boot could be supplemented by folding the rear seats to form an additional luggage area.

The bodywork was painted in powder blue with side panels of grey decorated with a regular pattern of thousands of hand painted four-leafed clovers. Internally the car was trimmed with grey-blue lizard skin in place of wood veneer.

## 1953 – *Silver Flash*

This car bore a strong overall resemblance to *Blue Clover*. At the rear the sloping boot had sprouted small fins, which were appearing on a number of road and racing cars at that time – e.g. the Bentley Continental and the Lotus 10. The conventional Daimler grille was replaced with a blended aperture, which strongly resembles the grille on the Daimler V8-250 of nine years later. This was flanked by two deeply recessed air intakes and the same Perspex glazed headlight arrangement as on the 1951 and 1952 cars. A fixed glass panel over the front seats incorporated an internal blind.

The two-seater coupe was initially painted dark green. Very shortly before the car made its first appearance the colour was quite understandably rejected by Lady Docker who felt that it looked too heavy. According to her account she decided on the new colour, metallic silver, and the car's name, which made reference to another famous BSA group product – their 650 cc Gold Flash motorbike. The interior trim was in black leather with red piping while the dashboard and other normally wood veneered areas were covered with red dyed crocodile skin. A matching pair of crocodile suitcases were installed behind the seats.

Soon after being sold by Daimler, *Silver Flash* was exported to the USA by its new owner Gordon Lieffring. Sitting behind the wheel he provides a sense of scale illustrating that, by the usual standards of the Docker Daimlers, this was quite a modest creation. (Al Lieffring)

*Above left*: *Silver Flash* of 1953. A fine example of what happens when you employ a professional designer. Few could have matched Hooper's chief designer Osmond Rivers for his ability to create such a bold 'Jet Age' shape, all scoops and intakes, while managing to evoke the cycle winged sports models of the early 1930s. (Al Lieffring)

*Above right*: When show time came round there was no telling which fauna would find themselves donating their hides for decorative effect. In this case, crocodiles. (Al Lieffring)

*Below*: Fins. Daimler seem to have had a bit of thing about them but without seeming to know why. These were said to aid directional stability, although it is unlikely the design ever saw the inside of a wind tunnel to find out if they did. (Al Lieffring)

Doubt has somehow arisen as to what type of chassis was used for this car, not helped by the fact that its whereabouts are unknown. The chassis number, 85001, indicates a prototype Conquest chassis. However, scaling off from photographs suggests a wheelbase of 114 ft, which supports contemporary reports describing it as a 'Daimler Special Series chassis' fitted with a three litre engine – i.e. probably a Daimler DF302 chassis.

## 1954 – *Stardust*

This car was built on the first Daimler DK400 chassis which was very slightly shorter and narrower than the later chassis in this series. The body design closely resembled the *Gold Car*, i.e. Empress-style limousine with twin headlights under Perspex covers. The bodywork was painted blue with the side panels hand painted with thousands of tiny silver stars.

A fixed glass panel over the rear seats could be covered by a motorised internal blind while the side windows were double glazed and motorised. The boot contained four suitcases in blue crocodile skin.

The rear compartment was trimmed with silver silk brocatelle while areas normally covered with wood veneer were trimmed with pale blue crocodile skin. The central division contained a drinks cabinet and what amounted to a very upmarket picnic set. The front compartment was trimmed in blue leather with grey piping. The dashboard was covered with crocodile matching that in the rear.

Something of a retreat to conventionality with 1954's *Stardust*. The wow factor resided in the craftsmanship and, once again, the man who was good at painting stars was given gainful employment. (Jaguar Daimler Heritage Trust)

# 1955 – *Golden Zebra*

Built on a Daimler DK400 chassis, this car had front panelwork that followed the lines of the standard Hooper limousine. The headlamps were cowled in the manner of that car, though somewhat more dramatically. From the b-post back the body was that of a two door coupe; rather high and slab sided with a lengthy boot. The body was painted a bright white and all of the brightwork was gold plated. The tyres were visually tied in with the use of whitewalls. The radiator shell was topped by a gold-plated zebra mascot.

Inside the cabin all of the brightwork was gold plated. The headlining was specially woven in ivory coloured cloth with small gold spots. The seats provided the explanation of the car's name as they were all trimmed with real zebra skins because mink, apparently the obvious alternative, feels too hot and moults. Or so it does according to Lady Docker who, it must be admitted, was one of very few people at the time who could pronounce on this subject with authority. The environmentalist's nightmare was completed by dashboard switches with knobs made from real ivory.

The interior was fitted out like some sort of mobile boudoir. Aside from the usual cocktail and picnic items which this time included Thermos flasks and (somewhat incongruously) Perspex sandwich boxes, there was a fitted manicure set, mirror, clothes brush and comb, powder compact, cigarette case and cream jar, as well as an ivory handled umbrella. The boot contained leather suitcases.

Perhaps surprisingly for such a dramatically styled car, *Golden Zebra* did generate one order from HH the Ameer of Bahawalpur for a similar DK400 based car. The Ameer's car differed in that it was a four door and the roof was made entirely from Perspex. The trim was fairly conventional, being in cream leather and birds-eye maple. Similarly styled bodywork was also ordered by separate customers for at least a couple of Rolls-Royce Silver Wraiths.

With nothing to provide a sense of scale, *Golden Zebra* might initially seem modestly sized although it was constructed on a chassis normally used for seven seater limousines. (Louwman Museum, The Hague, The Netherlands)

It is evidence of how avant-garde Hooper could be at this time that this dramatic design was very similar, from this viewpoint, to that of the standard DK400 based Hooper limousine. (Louwman Museum, The Hague, The Netherlands)

Daimler did not normally go in for mascots but *Golden Zebra* of 1955 was probably too good a chance to miss. (Louwman Museum, The Hague, The Netherlands)

Ivory and zebra skin covered almost everywhere between the floor and the roof, so it was just as well for the fauna of Africa that this Docker Daimler would turn out to be the last. (Louwman Museum, The Hague, The Netherlands)

## Aftermath

After the departure of the Dockers from BSA the cars were all disposed of to private buyers with most ending up in the USA. The *Gold Car* and *Golden Zebra* had their brightwork re-plated with chromium in order to comply with UK laws regarding the export of gold, and were given new paint, which rendered them relatively anonymous. Currently, all of the cars reside either in museums or with private collectors outside the UK. A Daimler DE36 with a body of the Green Goddess type is in the ownership of the Jaguar Heritage Trust at their base within the British Motor Museum at Gaydon in Warwickshire.

# 19

# Daimler after the Jaguar Takeover

By the late 1950s Jaguar were expanding fast and needed more production space. Due to restrictions imposed by government regional planning policy, any new factory would have to be built in what were then termed 'depressed areas', which effectively meant the north of England and Scotland. This was unattractive to Jaguar because widely spaced facilities would be inherently inefficient.

The Coventry area at this time was still home to a number of car manufacturers, which opened up an alternative route to expansion for Jaguar; if they could purchase an existing car factory near the city the government policy could be circumvented. Fortunately BSA were keen to shed Daimler, which was now one distraction too many in a group with too many other issues to deal with such as increasing motorcycle imports. In June 1960 Sir William Lyons purchased Daimler for £3.11 million, which provided him with Daimler's factory in Radford, only three miles from his Jaguar plant in Allesley.

Whilst the main point of acquiring the Daimler company was gaining a huge increase in production space right on Jaguar's doorstep, the Daimler brand had additional value to Jaguar. Marrying the technically brilliant but slightly flashy Jaguar to the oldest name in the industry gave them a credibility in the luxury market that they rather lacked.

At the time of the takeover, leaving aside non-car production such as the Ferret scout car and the Fleetline bus, Daimler were producing in very small numbers the Majestic, Majestic Major and SP250 models. Given how little money they were making and their quite significant shortcomings it is surprising how long Lyons kept these models in production. In 1962 the Daimler version of the Jaguar Mk 2 was the first indication of Daimler's future as an upmarket trim option. The V8 250 did at least have the 2.5 litre V8 engine developed by Daimler themselves. Later Daimler models, however, were no more than re-grilled and re-badged versions of their Jaguar counterparts. There were some high points, such as the Daimler DS420 limousine, based on the Jaguar 420G floorpan and running gear, which had no Jaguar equivalent, but otherwise the Daimler brand was gradually allowed to wither away.

The engineering excellence of cars such as the E-type and especially the XJ6 / XJ12 range wiped away Jaguar's previously rather flashy reputation. As the Jaguar brand became increasingly admired the Daimler brand became correspondingly irrelevant. When the

The DS420 was entirely a Jaguar creation, being based on the floorpan and running gear of their 420G. It deserves a mention here because it was the last Daimler that was not merely a trim variant of a Jaguar. (Soufiane El kadaoui, Wikimedia Commons)

XJ40 appeared in 1986 the fluted grille of the home market Daimler version was used in the USA for the highest spec Vanden Plas model. Both in this market and in Europe the Daimler name was increasingly being confused with Daimler Benz, which pleased neither Jaguar nor the makers of Mercedes Benz motor cars. The last Daimler, a Super Eight from the X350 range, was produced in 2007.

There was never any thought given by Jaguar to reviving the Lanchester brand, although a holding company, Lanchester Motor Company Limited, which they acquired as part of the takeover, still exists along with Daimler in the hands of Tata Motors, who are the present owners of Jaguar.

# 20

# Choosing a Daimler and Living With It

## Affordability

Although Daimlers are arguably undervalued, purchase price is going to define the available options for most people. The next consideration is accommodation. Daimlers do not take well to living outdoors and arrangements will need to be made for undercover storage. A Conquest or LD10 is going to fit in any normal lock-up; a DE36 however won't get much more than its bonnet through the doorway.

Fuel consumption is almost immaterial but do not underestimate the thirst of the larger models, which even the motorists of the 1950s would have seen as being on the wrong side of incredible. Most models can achieve about 25 mpg but for a DK400, for example, consumption in the order of 10 miles per gallon should not be unexpected.

The cost of parts is a trickier factor to weigh up since you can only have a limited idea of what you are going to need next. These are all old cars and any major component could in theory fail at any moment, and even lesser issues may arise in quick succession or hardly

A DLOC event will obviously attract a variety of Daimlers and Lanchesters, but even a small general classic show might field a surprising range of models. (Author)

at all. Apart from the V8 models the post-war cars are essentially variations of each other and even use a lot of identical components, so there is not much to distinguish one model from another in terms of maintenance costs. New replacement parts are being made, though not to anything like the extent of those for, say, Jaguars. They do, however, tend to be reasonably priced and very well made.

## Drivability

The chances are that you will want a car you can drive and therefore you should make an effort before buying a Daimler to try a few. Making approaches to owners at any regular car show should at least enable you to try out the driver's seat. Automotive speed dating might well open your eyes to unconsidered possibilities but it will also help avoid entanglements that are doomed to bitter failure. As excellently written as the chapter describing the pre-selector transmission is it is no substitute for an experience that you might enjoy or you might not. The day you collect that DB18 you won on eBay is not the time to find out.

As for checking the condition of what is there, you may investigate a likely purchase according to the guidance given below. In offering this guidance it is generally assumed that the reader has some knowledge of older cars and so does not need general advice such as how to check shock absorbers.

When inspecting a car for possible purchase you will need to make an assessment of not only the condition of what is there, but also the cost of obtaining later what is not. (Author)

# Chassis Frame

Most models described in this book are based on chassis that have no really significant mud and water traps and commonly bear little more than cosmetic rusting. The chassis number is stamped on a brass plate riveted to the top of the right hand chassis rail just before it heads off under the bulkhead. The chassis number is repeated, often with the engine number, on a plate on the bulkhead inside the engine bay. Both plates are also stamped with the chassis type – e.g. DJ260.

The chassis plate is awkward to get sight of and, as this picture shows, can be difficult to read even when it is not covered with oil and road dirt. (Author)

The chassis number is repeated on the bulkhead, either with another chassis plate or one of these identification plates. In this case the car is on a chassis type DJ260 – i.e. Daimler Conquest automatic. (Author)

## Engines

The in-line engines are rather unexciting but sturdy units. The V8 engines are exciting, or at least a lot of people get excited about them, but again fundamentally reliable.

## Fuel System

Most cars were fitted with a fuel reserve valve operated from the dashboard by a Bowden cable of quite extraordinary length. If the valve's cork seals fail, fuel will leak through the valve body and drain the fuel tank out onto the floor. New seals are available.

A similar issue arises with the H6 carburettor used up to 1955. This has cork jet seals in the base which can dry out and shrink during periods of idleness, again giving rise to a fuel leak, this time directly over the exhaust pipe. The HD6 which superseded the H6 has a jet mounted on a flexible diaphragm which should be taken out, checked thoroughly for any sign of cracking and replaced unless it is in absolutely perfect condition.

## Cooling System

All Daimlers have cooling systems, which are perfectly adequate, whatever anyone who sells electric cooling fans for a living may tell you. If your Daimler overheats the most likely cause is sludge and rust scale in the cooling passages within the engine block. The cure is to clear this all out and then use rust-inhibiting anti-freeze, as the previous owners should have but obviously did not.

## Gearbox

See Chapter Three concerning the pre-selector transmission. The only alternative was the Borg-Warner automatic gearbox, which is a reliable unit. Gearbox mounts are well

The rubber in gearbox mounts can suffer horribly from oil that has leaked from the engine or gearbox. (Author)

positioned to gather oil leaking from the engine and gearbox, which softens the rubber so that the gearbox is no longer held firm. The gearbox cannot fall down but it may be able to move enough to make gear selection difficult. Mounts for all the post-war models are available brand new and fitting is very straightforward.

## Suspension and Axles

Although various front suspension layouts were used, they were all quite conventional examples of their type and have no particular weak points. An important point to note is that sulphur-based oils must not be used in worm drive axles – e.g. DB18 – as they will destroy the phosphor-bronze gears.

## Self-Lubrication

Most models, until the mid-1950s, were fitted with an automatic lubrication system, which served the suspension and steering joints. This consisted of an oil reservoir connected via a pump unit by pipes to the various lubrication points. The pump unit was a sealed container situated next to the exhaust down pipe. Heat from the exhaust caused the oil to expand; one-way valves in the pump connections meant that the warm oil was forced to leave the pump down the pipe to the lubrication points. When the engine was turned off the oil in the pump cooled and contracted, thus creating a vacuum that drew in a top-up from the reservoir. Operation of the system can be checked by loosening the lubrication points and checking that they are weeping oil. The really important point is to not confuse the oil reservoir with the brake fluid reservoir. Always check before topping up either that you are really sure which is which.

## Brakes

Most models up to the DK400 were fitted with some form of at least partly mechanical braking system. Properly set up they work well; however, whilst these are very simple systems, there are key aspects of assembly and adjustment which can confuse and confound those unfamiliar with them. Do not attempt to work on the brakes without first studying the relevant technical literature.

## Bodywork

Bodies are of two sorts. The higher volume models carry bodies of welded pressed steel construction, which offer all the usual potential for rotting out. Coachbuilt bodies are a joy to everyone except the poor souls who have to repair them. The chief issue is decay of the ash framing, which is hard to access under the panels it was intended to support. Also, coachbuilt panels such as doors and bootlids from a donor car will rarely fit another car without considerable reworking. These inconsistencies aside, bodies were made to a high standard, so if anything does not look or feel right then find out why. Check for close and even panel gaps and firmness of attachment for any hinged panels.

Daimler doors are especially prone to rusting because they were not fitted with sealing rubbers against the bottom of the wind-up windows and placed total reliance on drain holes in the bottom of the doors to keep them dry inside. In practice the doors don't often flood because the bottoms rust out.

All bodywork ahead of the windscreen (apart from on the SP250 and V8-250) is bolted on, which means that second-hand parts are more available than they might be since it is easier to recover them from a scrap car than it would be if they were welded in place. Front valances are very prone to rusting out.

## Glass

Front windscreens especially may be held in place by metal retaining tabs obscurely installed in a seemingly ad-hoc fashion. If you have trouble removing a screen you would do well to check before assuming that it is simply stuck to the rubber seal and just needs a firm thump.

## Brightwork

Chrome was applied with restraint, although the bumpers on the DK and Majestic ranges in particular are enormous, as is the cost of re-plating them.

Cast brightwork such as door handles is generally made from a zinc-based alloy known as mazac or zamac. Under either name it is horrible stuff. Most such components will exhibit some corrosion in the form of swollen scabs, which eventually fall away leaving

A typical example of corrosion in a mazac moulding. There is a fix that involves grinding out the rot and filling it with solder before re-plating. It is akin to precision dentistry and is not cheap. (Author)

deep pitting. Most platers will not touch the stuff and the best advice is to seek out good second-hand replacements, although reproduction door handles for the Lanchester Fourteen / Leda and Daimler Conquest ranges are occasionally available.

## Interior Trim

As with windscreens, removal of interior trim from a Daimler can be surprisingly involved. A Daimler Conquest front door trim, for example, is fixed with twenty screws and sixteen spring clips.

Leather seat covers are rarely given the care they need resulting in seats that are as hard as concrete because the leather has been allowed to dry out. This can often be cured by intensive feeding and regular cleaning thereafter with saddle soap. The one thing you must not do is sit on any seat where the leather has dried out, because in that state it will be extremely brittle and prone to splitting.

## Technical Literature

A handbook was produced for every model, even the Sprite. These contain a great deal of information about the operation and maintenance of the vehicle, which is supplemented by the well illustrated official parts lists. The only workshop manual that Daimler issued was for the Daimler Conquest range. Jaguar produced parts lists and workshop manuals for the V8 models after their takeover in 1960. Much of this factory literature has been issued on CD by the Jaguar Heritage Trust.

When the cars were new the trade magazine *Motor Trader* produced service data sheets – in effect a miniature workshop manual – for the Lanchester LD10 and Fourteen / Leda, the Daimler DB18 / Consort and the Conquest range, as well as a couple covering the Jaguar Mk 2, which would be of use to owners of the Daimler V8-250. Some useful information can be had from the trade catalogues and technical literature put out by component suppliers such as Lucas (electrical equipment), Wilmot Breeden (door catches), and Girling (braking). Lubrication service charts for all models were produced by Shell and Esso.

Finally there are two clubs that are each in their own way a useful resource. The Daimler & Lanchester Owners Club (www.dloc.org.uk and info@dloc.org.uk) offers all the services one would expect of a large well-established club, including a monthly glossy newsletter, regular local and national meets and shows, and access to model specialists. The club also maintains an internet forum (http://forum.dloc.co.uk), accessible by non-members, which is an excellent source of advice and information about all Daimler, Lanchester, and BSA cars.

The Daimler Enthusiasts Club (www.daimlerclub.co.uk and enquiries@daimlerclub. co.uk) is a rather different animal, which, although it does produce a quarterly newsletter, mainly restricts its activities to the supply of second-hand and remanufactured parts for cars from the 1945–60 period.

# Bibliography

Bird, Anthony & Hutton-Stott, Francis, *Lanchester Motor Cars, A History* (London, Cassell, 1965)

Smith, Brian E., *The Daimler Tradition* (Isleworth, Transport Bookman Publications, 1980)

Lord Montagu of Beaulieu, *Lost Causes of Motoring* (London, Cassell, 1966)

Nixon, St. John C., *Daimler 1896 to 1946, 50 Years of the Daimler Company* (London, G. T. Foulis & Co. Ltd, 1946)

Speed, John F., *British Motor Cars* (London, G. T. Foulis & Co. Ltd, 1952)

Mynard, Dennis & Wilson, Harold, *Daimler Conquest Roadster and New Drophead Coupe* (Port Talbot, privately published, 2014)

Freeman, Tony & Long, Brian & Hood, Chris, *Lanchester Cars 1895–1956* (London, Academy Books, 1990)

McHattie J. N., *Servicing Guide to British Motor Vehicles, Vols. 1 & 2* (London, Trader Publishing Co., 1953)

Moss A. J. K., *Servicing Guide to British Motor Vehicles, Vol. 3* (London, Trader Publishing Co., 1955)

Docker, Lady Norah, *Norah, the autobiography of Lady Docker* (London, W. H. Allen & Co. Ltd, 1969)

Townsin, Alan, *Ian Allan Transport Library:Daimler* (Shepperton, Ian Allan Publishing, 2000)

Munro, Bill, *Carbodies, The Complete Story* (Marlborough, The Crowood Press Ltd, 1998)

Young, Daniel, *Daimler Digest, DB18 and Conquest Ranges (1945–1957)* (London, P4 Spares, 1990)

Thorley, Nigel, *Jaguar, All The Cars 2nd Edition* (Yeovil, Haynes Publishing, 2009)

Robson, Graham, *The Cars of BMC* (Epsom, Motor Racing Publications, 1986)

Sedgwick, Michael & Gillies, Mark, *Classic & Sportscar – A-Z of Cars 1945–1970* (Twickenham, Temple Press, 1986)

L. A. Mainwaring, *The Observer's Book of Automobiles* (London, Frederick Warne & Co., 1962)